THE ULTIMATE RELATIONSHIP
PART 1

RIA SARAH

The Ultimate Relationship

- Part 1 -

Ria Sarah

The Ultimate Relationship: Part I

Copyright © 2018 Ria Sarah

First published 2018

Publisher: MJL Publications

17 Spencer Avenue
Deception Bay QLD 4508
Australia

WEB: www.mjlpublications.com.au

All rights reserved. Without limiting the rights under copyright reserved above, no part of this publication may be reproduced, stored in or introduced in to a database and retrieval system, or transmitted in any form or by any means (electronic, mechanical, photocopying, recording or otherwise) without the prior written permission of both the owner of the copyright and the above publishers.

ISBN# 978-0-6483778-3-2

Table of Contents

Chapter 1: Childhood 7

Chapter 2: Perfect Child No More 15

Chapter 3: Shattered Plans 27

Chapter 4: Being a member of a Church 39

Chapter 5: Married at Eighteen 47

Chapter 6: Marriage Not Going to Plan 63

Chapter 7: Self-Sabotage in its Finest Form 79

Chapter 8: Running Away 97

Chapter 9: At the Retreat 127

Chapter 10: Life After the Retreat 147

Chapter 1: Childhood

Chapter 1: Childhood

So here it is! My book, MY STORY...

My first chapter is about the perfect child – well, being one, resembling one. Being the perfect child for me was being the eldest of three children. My mum did this on her own, and it was very hard on her emotionally & physically. Why? Because my dad was always in his bakery; that was his life, his job, but there was a lot going on behind the scenes, as it is always in his life.

Although I was very little, my dad left when I was 6. Then he divorced mum when I was 8. Yeah, yeah, this happens all the time these days. But this was my father, my family, and this is my story.

Around this time, I remember my mum getting ill. I remember her being in bed for a long time, days even. I remember her friend coming over and checking in on her. Her friend came and helped and got money withdrawn from mum's account, or maybe even it was even provided by her, I'm not sure.

From that moment I just took the reins of the family, in any way I could. I cooked, and I cleaned. I did a lot around the house for my younger brother and sister, also for mum. There wasn't anything in my mind that said I couldn't do this, I just did what I had to because somebody needed to do it and the job needed to be done. Like when I was 8 years old, the lawn was so long, right up to my knees. I don't know even know if she had the money, that wasn't even a thought that crossed my mind... we had a mower, and somebody needed to mow

Ultimate Relationship: Part 1

the lawn. I jumped on that and I taught myself how to mow the lawn, I had watched neighbours do it.

I absolutely loved mowing the lawn. I don't know whether I loved it more because the little old lady (bless her heart) next door used to offer a glass of lemonade and a bag of lollies after every time I finished it. She used to tell me how much of a good girl I was. It was instant gratification, and I still have that same feeling even today at 36 years of age whenever I mow the lawn. I absolutely love how it makes me feel, how I take my time to do a job that makes me proud.

So, I looked after the family. I did the lawns and I remember taking money with me, a $100.00 note, with my brother and sister when my mum was in bed, and we did the grocery shop. We walked 3 blocks away to where my Dad's shop still was at the time. We were getting the groceries at our local Jewel Supermarket. We got our groceries all together and carried them all the way home. Yep, the bags broke from the heaviness of the cans, but we all stuck together and got it done.

We also got to go to Christian Camps every Christmas holidays. I enjoyed these camps immensely. Had so many laughs, met so many nice people and filled up my pen-pal lists. Got to try out a flying fox and ride a 4x4 motorbike. These were great holidays.

Anyway, life just carried on as usual. Then, at the age of 12, my mum had located her birth mum. This was exciting news for my mum as she searched for her for years. We found out

Chapter 1: Childhood

that she belonged to a rather large family, she was one of seven. The news of my mum being found or vice versa quickly spread, and we ventured into this territory of meeting new family. We got a visit from her natural mum and her husband, which was such a memorable visit for me. What exactly was memorable? It just was. Actually, I think it was the first time I felt I truly belonged.

We also had a visit from my mum's younger sister. My mum had a sister – well actually, two. In her adoptive family she only had a brother. It was such a privilege to be introduced to new family which was ours, one that we call our own. They called us their own as well.

Life as we knew it was about to change dramatically. Mum made the decision based on a whole bunch of circumstances which was unknown to me (or I can't remember being told) to leave Sydney (Colyton) and move up to Kempsey. So, we painted the house, removed wall paper, tidied up the home for sale. Such a big job. Our family home of 12 years, Sold.

Off we went to Kempsey, and that's where we lived and created our new life. We lived in a friend's cottage whilst mum got started building her house the way she wanted; it was even pink. Pink Besser Brick. It seemed to take a while to build as there were hiccups with builders and council regulations. None the less, we carried on as usual.

We moved into this home and my mum's 'new' family came and visited us. The whole lot of them came to our home for a family reunion. It was amazing. It was like the family we had

Ultimate Relationship: Part 1

been searching for all our lives without even knowing. They rallied and worked with us. I think their assistance, for my mum, was the biggest gift I had the pleasure of watching my mum receive. This will be a memory that stays with me forever.

The roles of the family remained the same in a lot of ways. Mum got work in Kempsey in horticulture. Probably where my love for gardening came from. I continued to do lots around the house, like ironing, washing the clothes and bringing them in, cooking. Mum did such a fine job raising us kids, we always had shoes on our feet, food in the cupboards and fridges. We never went without, at least to my recollection.

However, my father came back on the scene. Whether he just came back on the scene or whether he just showed up... Not sure. I mean, mum never ever hid any communications about

Chapter 1: Childhood

him from us... I remember making phone calls to him from time to time. Some to ask for money – have no idea if any ever came – and other times calling him desperately, asking him to be in my life... I wanted my Daddy.

But he just rocked up one day, and he brought three of my sisters whom I knew nothing about at that time. Well, actually, I knew of one little girl that my dad had with another woman when I was eight. She was named Sara, and I know that my mum was extremely upset because that's my middle name. I didn't know why this caused her great pain but regardless of that she was my sister. So, they came to spend some time with us. I don't know how long that time was, maybe a week, I don't even know if it was that long. All I knew was that I went from having one sister to having four. These three were so small and ever so cute. They were Sara, Laura and Casey.

There was one birthday when I got a CD player from my Dad. I don't even know what year it was. It was the 'top notch' of technology back then. It had a double tape deck, and a five stack CD player, and I just remember having the biggest arguments with my siblings because I got this – for my birthday – and they didn't. I just got so angry and frustrated that I was like "Well, you have it." Anyway, that was my perspective at the time.

Dad seemed to engage more with me at this time and inviting me for trips – to come up and visit him, go to church, go to youth camps, stuff like that, which was good. I got to meet a whole bunch of new people whom I called my friends at the

Ultimate Relationship: Part 1

time. I guess one of the pivotal moments for me was when I was 15, and dad asked me if I wanted to come and live with him. I thought that would be great because I always wanted that connection with my dad. To me it was like a dream come true – 15 years of my life has passed and now my dad wanted to have a connection with his daughter. I couldn't believe my ears, I was so happy. Dad said that he would put $25 a fortnight into my account. I am not sure why he chose to do this. It provided snacks for me at school that mum didn't buy because we ate a preservative, colour, additive free diet. That was about to change, too.

However, mum was not impressed about that, so she said no. Her decision threw me for six! I just could not believe, after everything I had done, that I was being refused this one thing that I wanted to do.

I was so upset by this that I took matters into my own hands. I did what I wanted to do anyways. I changed friend groups at school. I started hanging out more with this other group. I started smoking in the toilet block with some of the girls. It was purely disgusting when I first tried it. I bum puffed as well and choked and coughed some more. That didn't stop me.

I had not long moved into the Public-School world after all my schooling in Private Schooling. It was one of the best things I could've ever done because it made me pull up my socks and step into my big girl shoes and stop allowing people to bully and tease me because of my name. The words stung my eyes every day for all my school life up until grade 8 when I moved

Chapter 1: Childhood

school. Something started to change within me as all the names that I had been called every day of my school life started to stop. I still heard Diarrhea, Gonorrhoea, Retard, Airhead or Stinky (Stengert was my maiden name), but it was like this wall came up around me. If I heard them at the public high school, I felt like I would just shrug them off.

Chapter 2: Perfect Child No More

Chapter 2: Perfect Child No More

I'd been asked to go and live with my father and my mother wouldn't let me. So, when my mother wouldn't let me leave Kempsey, I don't know, I felt like asking, "How dare you?" because I'd never did. I'd done everything I could to be that perfect person.

I wouldn't know the reasons why until later; however, that just threw me for a spin. I started smoking, hanging out with different people, I dabbled with a bit of pot. I used to buy little $10.00 foils. That's how we used to buy them back in the day, we used to get $10 foils of marijuana leaf, bud or head. Leaf was the cheapest you could buy, and we used to go through our lunch breaks, sometimes through class, and go over behind the hospital and sit on the hillside and have a little bit of a toke.

I hated every minute of it. I really disliked it, but I did it because I felt included, and I guess in some space of my mind when I was not allowed to do what I wanted to do I felt excluded in some way. So, I looked for that extra outlet. Then drinking came into it. I had this great supply of money, you see, because of the $25 a fortnight that my father used to supply me. I don't remember why he was giving it to me, he never gave it to my siblings, that I know of.

Back in the mid '90s, you were able to purchase a pack of cigarettes for about $6, which I was able to – I was just under 16, and the legal age back then was 16. You could also buy a bottle of bombora, which was a cheap alcohol at $9.99. I used to drink it with milk. That was my drink of choice, and my dad

Ultimate Relationship: Part 1

used to supply me the means to do what I wanted to do without even knowing it.

It introduced me to a whole new world as it gave me, in some way, a false sense of confidence and a new skill set of confidence all at the same time. Where once I wasn't strong enough to stand up to people and tell them to fuck off whenever they would tease me, all of a sudden, I had this new skill set where I had that ability to let them know that I've heard it all before and there's nothing they can say that's going to hurt me anymore. I had been hurt over and over again by many people, but I was becoming stronger every day. I find there are times in our life where we just build our walls up. That's what I did.

A moment that stood out for me was the first party I went to, where there was anything and everything in the world of drugs and alcohol. As I was the newbie, everything was offered to me... and I tasted it. Port, yuck! Spat that stuff straight out. Wine... Yuck! Spat it out. To be honest, I tried many things and was not the least bit sober at the end of the evening.

What really stuck out in my mind was when I was lying in this tent with this guy I had just met that evening. Right beside me was my best friend and her boyfriend. I was very new to this whole guy/girl thing – what it was, what was involved. I remember lying there on my back, and the hard ground beneath me was very uncomfortable. Here was this guy lying on top of me. He was doing this thing with his tongue and I remember thinking, "Really? Is this what it's all about?" I felt

Chapter 2: Perfect Child No More

like a dog. He was licking my face like a dog laps its water out of a bowl. And my friend was like, "If you go the whole way, I will too", or something similar. My mind was boggling, probably from the pot, but also from the ridiculous situation I was in. No freakin' way was I doing anything more with this guy. Yuck.

This didn't end there. You see this guy had a girlfriend, and they parted ways the day before or maybe even that day. I had no clue but was about to find out. The very next day when I went to school as usual, I got off my bus and was walking into the school grounds when I heard, "Ria you SLUT!" being yelled out of the bus on its way to the high school up the road. Whoa!

Oops, high school students came up to me and told me why this chick was yelling obscenities. I stole her boyfriend. I laughed at the very thought. I had done no such thing. Period. She can have him. The very thought of pursuing anything with this guy made me sick. But this chick was hearing none of it! She was out for the kill. She was stalking my every move. She found out when I was in her suburb and rocked up on my friend's doorstep. I still don't know how she found out, but also don't care now either. I had just finished smoking some pot with my girlfriend and I had the munchies, and I was eating the only thing in the house – Vegemite and Vita-Weats. Feral to say the least. I hate Vegemite! My girlfriend answered the door and said, "Sam was here". What the hell?!? She was here to make peace with me. Oh, that's ok then, "Yeah, of course." She said, "Can we go for a walk and talk?" Me being me, "Yes, of course." Off I went.

Ultimate Relationship: Part 1

We walked down the street past about 3 houses and she was being very pleasant. We walk around the corner and then BANG! She punches me straight in the nose and this sheering pain is running through my head. Tears pour down my face and she is standing there yelling at me. I can't hear the words she is yelling at me, all I can feel is pain and utter shock as this was meant to be a peaceful talk. I looked at her and then ran. She yelled louder and louder. I was a very fast runner through school, getting to state finals, etc. I ran back to my friend's place and she didn't come after me. Phew…

Another friend invited me to another party with older people, guys. They were out of school. I remember saying to my girlfriend that afternoon while smoking a cigarette, "I think tonight is the night. I won't be a virgin by the end of night." Oh, we laughed and giggled. How I wished I could have taken back those words for many years to come.

The night was going well. I had my bombora, drinking it very steadily. Talking to a friend of the guy that lived at the house. I thought he was really nice. And how I wish he had taken me that night to wherever he stayed, as it would have been far better than what took place. You see, I was still the newbie, the virgin. Everyone seemed to know this, or at least I felt as though it was imprinted on my head or something. Keep drinking, keep drinking… my insecurities disappeared and there I was, drunk beyond all capacity, sitting on the sofa on the balcony of this place. I couldn't move, I couldn't talk.

Chapter 2: Perfect Child No More

Then something happened, and still to this day, I don't know whether I passed out or fell asleep, but it doesn't really matter. What happened next got embedded in my memory for the rest of my life. When I came to, I found myself lying on the tennis green fake grass, completely naked, this guy on top of me. This wasn't the guy I had been talking to earlier in the evening. This was someone completely different. Who was he? Yet here he was, pumping on top of me, I was screaming but no words escaped my mouth. What the hell was going on? I could see all these people still standing around drinking, like I was invisible, maybe I was. They didn't even seem bothered by what was going on right below their noses. I could hear them laughing and carrying on, but why couldn't they hear me? I remember lying there and hearing my friend say, "Is that Ria?" She had her head out the doorway and looking in my direction. "Yes!" I shouted out to her, "Come and get me!" My screams went unheard again. This was unbearable.

I shut off and awoke the next morning in a lounge room, with clothes on. I sat up slowly, feeling like my head was too explode. There were some guys in the lounge room, they were snickering. I asked them what they were snickering about. They said to go and look in the mirror. Off I went to the bathroom. OH my gosh! My neck was black and blue, like I mean black and blue. Hickies, I was told. What the hell happened last night?

All I knew was that I had to hide my neck from my mum and the kids at school. So middle of summer I am wearing a turtle neck skivvy right up under my chin. Nooo, this wasn't obvious

Ultimate Relationship: Part 1

at all. I don't remember if my mum ever saw this or made comment, it didn't matter. I had bigger eggs to fry. You see, the very next day, that chick was yelling "SLUT" to me again. Now I was really confused. Really? Why now? I clearly was the last to know. Kids from hangouts were talking to me and telling me how I slept with Simon last night. I don't know how they knew, or what happened but it was like I "made the cut". I was being invited everywhere.

Next Invite, I was back at the house where I spoke to that really nice guy. We went to another party and he was offering me some Bacardi. I was swigging it back, ouch! It burnt all the down, then was all warm and fuzzy. He wanted to leave, and I went with him. We got in the car and we were kissing. We arrived at a house but didn't stop kissing. He was kissing me very differently to how I had been kissed up until this point. It was really nice. Up the stairs to the unit, and we stopped on the platform of the stairwell as the kissing got really intense. Our shirts came off. Completely swept up in the moment, the tenants of the house came home and laughed as they walk past us. We continued, and I seemed unbothered by anything at this point.

The stairs were carpeted, and all our clothes came off and there I am, lying in a stairwell of this house again, and next thing I knew something was shoved in my mouth – his dick. My eyes almost boggled out of my head. He looked at me and said, "Suck it." He put his hand to the back of head and was thrusting himself into my mouth. I was gagging. This was

Chapter 2: Perfect Child No More

awful. Do guys really expect girls to do this? I can't remember the rest of this night. My mind went into shutdown and quite frankly I forgot about all my memories from this house until many years later.

It got to the point the binge parties were getting a little bit out of control and I'd slept with a few guys. So much changed in this 6-month period: I was being told I was reckless and that I didn't listen.

I didn't realize it at that time, as I thought I was just having fun, but looking back I can see the recklessness in it. I didn't really give a shit about myself. I knew one thing for sure, and that was that I was getting really good at throwing myself in the spotlight with men and not giving a fuck what they did to me. I was loving the attention that I was getting. I hated the concept of people telling me to love myself, when they wouldn't tell me how. I did it the best way I could with what I had, and that's all I could do.

Another of those pivotal moments was when I had been over behind the hospital and had a joint of my leaf marijuana and then come back to my history class. Probably not my best decision...

This teacher wasn't exactly the best teacher. We all know we have teachers that really come from the dark ages, but my teacher really took the cake. Basically, I was sitting on my chair facing the front of the class room, but the back of my chair was facing the side of the classroom. For whatever reason this teacher decided to pick on me that day, and he wanted me to

Ultimate Relationship: Part 1

move my chair. Unbeknownst to me, there's many underlying reasons why I acted the way I did; however, being under the influence of pot (marijuana) I had no inhibitions, and I acted the only way I knew how. He came near me to move the chair and touched my arm. I literally screamed at him, "Fuck off! You will not touch me."

Obviously, that started a commotion within the classroom because nobody had heard me speak, ever, as I was the shy girl all through my schooling up until just recently. The one who just cried or got called names. I just never spoke a word, and when I literally let loose on this teacher all the guys in the classroom were cheering me on, wolf-whistling. In that moment, I felt validated to an extent, because here I was standing up for myself.

I was really mad at the teacher for doing what he did; and yet, this is how we become strong, maybe not in the way that I did it, but this is how we become confident, by having our ways validated. Anyway, back to the point, the teacher was extremely pissed off as he was caught off guard as well, and he reacted the only way you do when you have that kind of reaction in front of you and you react back, so he yelled at me, "Get out of my classroom!" and pointed to the door, and so I went and sat outside the classroom as we did in those days, but he said "NO. I want you upstairs in front of the history department staffroom." I think that's what it was called. So, I went up there for remainder of the class, then I got sent to the principal's office, then I got a suspension notice. Suspended for 3 days. Holy Shit!

Chapter 2: Perfect Child No More

I thought of how all the ways I could work out how my mum was not going to find out about this because I thought: here I am, the child that does no wrong, I can't let her know that I've done something like this. This was the worst thing ever.

So, I worked out a little plan for how to keep it from her. The principal had given me a copy and sent one home to my mum. At that time, my sister was at home sick, so when I got home I asked her if she could get the letter for me. Mobile phones didn't exist back then, which probably worked in my favour. I asked her to retrieve it, rip it up and throw it in the bin, which either she or I may have done. So long ago. I was grateful. So, for the next few days I just 'attended school as normal', except I was wearing casual clothing underneath my school uniform. My days would then be filled with hanging out at friends of friends and smoking pot, eating munchy food and listening to music.

Whether or not my mum knew about this I'm not really sure to this day, she never really mentioned it; however, the three days turned into two weeks and I end up having to tell her so that I could go back to school. So, I obviously told her, and then we had to have an interview with the principal, talk about what I'd done, and that I'm not going to do again, blah blah blah...

Everything escalated from that point. There was pot, there was drinking, there was even dabbling with painkillers to see what they would do if I took a whole tray. I remember taking a whole tray of Panadol and being in English class, and I

Ultimate Relationship: Part 1

actually hated my English teacher, he just reminded me of Santa Claus – not that every Santa Claus is a horrible person – but I just disliked him. He used to scream, he didn't teach he'd just lecture, and I didn't really learn anything from his teachings, so this day I jumped out the window.

It wasn't far, it was only on the first level of a very old school building, but I jumped out that window on that class. I tripped and fell on the way to the bus and had blood pouring out of my knee and I didn't even care. Apparently, I was high as a kite on Panadol.

I did a bunch of stuff. It basically got to the point where my friends were very worried about me and wrote a letter to me. At the time it was an anonymous letter, but it was from a friend of mine whom I am still in contact with today. She wrote a letter saying something like this (but in so many more words):

"I know things about you, and I know what you're doing. You're being extremely reckless, and if you don't make a decision to stop now I'm going to tell your mum everything."

I read that letter and it pissed me off that somebody could betray my trust like that. However, at the same time, it was the next pivotal moment for me. I literally made another decision: to just go. After I contemplated the letter, I just went to my mum and said, "I'm going, there is no ifs or buts about this now. I contacted my dad and told him I'm coming."

Chapter 2: Perfect Child No More

It all happened so fast, and next thing I knew I was at a tiny petrol station in Kempsey with my bag of luggage and my box of belongings and that was it. When mum took me to the bus station she disclosed a few things about her marriage, which I thought was completely inappropriate at the time because she had full opportunity to tell me about these things before I left, and yet here I was with the bus ticket to go and visit the person that she was disclosing all this information about. However, it didn't seem to shift my decision in moving, so off I went.

Chapter 3: Shattered Plans

Chapter 3: Shattered Plans

I moved up to Queensland.

It wasn't the pretty picture that I had created in my own head. The plan was going to look like this: me, having this relationship with my father, and it being the best thing in the world and he was going to dote on me as he missed out on so many years together. I was going to have my Daddy back. This was my forever dream. I was going to be in this loving daddy-daughter relationship for the first time ever. I was so looking forward to it.

Yeah, my dreams crashed and burned really, really quickly. This wasn't in my dad's plan for me. He wanted me to go to a private school, and I didn't really want to go to a private school. After all the years of private schooling I had been kept down a grade, even though I moved from grade 10 to grade 10 across the states, I was bored shitless.

I did as Dad wanted and I went to this private school doing grade 10 and it was everything that I learned in grade 9 in New South Wales. I asked my dad if I could move to the public high school because it had more subjects that I was interested in, and it was also a much cheaper option. Nope. He blatantly told me no, so I thought of another way to get what I wanted and that was to go to TAFE. My dad gave me two options: either go to TAFE and leave school or continue in grades 11 and 12 at the private Christian school. The private school was not an option for me, so I left and went to TAFE. That was the start of me getting on my own feet and starting all over again, or so I thought.

Ultimate Relationship: Part 1

The pretty picture that I had planned for this great father-daughter time was being shattered over and over again. It just wasn't as I had pictured it.

The living arrangement changed dramatically after I moved up to live with my father. My dad got a girlfriend. That just upset me to no end. Here I was, I missed out on all these years of this father time and he was putting all his energy into this woman, and I just couldn't understand it. I was 15 and just moved to another state, I knew barely anyone but a few people at church because I had to attend the church with my father. Life started to spin.

One particular night stands out: was when my dad was about to go to his Men's Bible study group and he wanted to have a talk. I am not sure of any events that took place prior to this conversation.

He was sitting on his lounge in his study, and I was on his swivel computer chair at his desk. He started accusing me of things, things I had not said let alone thought of. He was just yelling "My girlfriend and I are not sleeping together" over and over again. My head hurt, and to many this may not seem like much. I couldn't understand why he was blaming me for saying things I had not said. My dad was really cross with me. I looked on the desk and found a nail file, and as my dad got louder and louder, I brought the nail file up to my chest and started to dig it in. I was holding it so tight between my rib cage, but it wouldn't bloody pierce the skin. Dad was still going on and on, it was like white noise by this stage as my heart

Chapter 3: Shattered Plans

hurt so bad. I just needed to stop the pain. I kept digging the nail file deeper.

Then he just stopped and said, "Ok, I am off to study. Dinner is in the kitchen." I couldn't look at him. My face was covered in tears and he wasn't going to see me like this. Off he went. The minute I heard his car leave the driveway, I got up out the chair. I sniffled and cleaned myself up a bit. I was mad, like livid mad. I went from hurting to utter rage. I had all these questions. Why? What made him say that? Did I really do something? Say something? Arrrgghhh. I wanted a smoke. It had been weeks since I had one, I had no money. So, I searched my father's house high and low. Oh, look at that, a coin collection, yay. So, I found all the coins that resembled Australian money and – knock knock.

Who the hell was at the door? The Pastor's wife and her daughters. What the Hell? My dad phoned them and was worried about me. He gave them a phoney story of why I was so upset, and I quickly ironed it out. All the good that did, they just 'prayed' for me. I sat in doorway crying and they sat with me. Who knows what they thought, but then they left.

I quickly took a walk to the local petrol station. It was about 7.30pm and it was dark, but I didn't care one bit. In fact, I had even thought that if I was grabbed they could do whatever they wanted. Nothing could hurt me the way my father just did. I got to the petrol station and got my smokes. Lucky the legal age back then was 16, I never got asked for ID. Walking home and smoking my cigarettes, suddenly my world started

Ultimate Relationship: Part 1

to calm down. I showered and went to bed. Nothing was ever mentioned again of that night or the conversation.

My dad then decided to tell me that I was going to have to move in with his girlfriend in her 3-bedroom townhouse because he was traveling for work and I needed to be looked after. It was not my best experience, to be honest. It was actually the worst living experience I ever had. I had come from living with my mum and being able to do everything, which I did, I did do most things. Cook, bake, wash when it needed to be done, iron and shop, even. Then I had to go to a place where I was being dictated to by this woman I hardly knew and being told when I could come down the stairs, when I could sit at the table, what I could eat for breakfast.

I grew to hate life, my life, very fast. I guess it was because I was a 15-year-old who had been given all this freedom to an extent because I was so adapted to my previous home, and then suddenly I was not allowed to make my own breakfast. Here I was, stuck in this household where I had to get ready in the morning for school as per usual and wait until she called me down like I was at a boarding school or something.

She was very routine orientated. This isn't a bad thing, but the way she 'inflicted' her ways upon me was. This was not for me. I wanted tomato on toast. When I ask for tomato on toast, I expect the toast to be warm, but it wasn't – it was cooked when... I don't know, half an hour before. Stone cold! I was thinking, "Oh my god," and I had to sit there and eat this bloody shit. Don't get me started on the milo she gave me. Or

Chapter 3: Shattered Plans

the 10-minute dinner that was cooked in the microwave. Yep. chicken schnitzel, sliced potato, and peas. Oh, and some white sauce. It was vile, but that's all I got. She covered hers in tomato sauce. I just told myself to eat it. This place was feeling more like hell every day, and this was the source of my food. Do what you have to do, Ria.

It was things like that which made my skin crawl. Then my dad proposed to her, and next thing they were getting married. They can do what they want, but just it crushed me even more, crushed my dreams minute by minute, hour by hour.

I got a little excited when I was asked to be the bridesmaid – not because they were getting married, but because I got to pick out a dress. I couldn't believe it when I found this gorgeous dress, fit like a glove, looked older than my years. I felt amazing. Shattered again, "No you're not wearing that," she said. I was churning on the inside. This woman was turning me inside out. "Nope, you can wear this one." Red and white polka dots. You have got to be joking! It was horrendous. I looked like an elephant in it, it was disgusting. That's what I was forced to wear. No, no physical chains in the forcing. Believe me, these were invisible ones.

So, then we all moved in together and played 'happy family'. This was short lived, as I was quickly learning. My Dad and his promises, not travelling anymore. Then off he goes. Promises, promises. Broken with every breath he takes.

Wow, when that happened I was just like, "Holy moly, this woman is just rocking my world because I'm not living under your rules." She was a rule unto herself. She quickly turned into one of those step mothers in those horror movies when Dad wasn't around.

I found myself in this place, living with this woman which I never planned on doing, and I don't know, she had some things going on for her, that's her story to tell not mine. However, for me, she invaded my privacy by going through my room. She'd go into my room, she would go through my things. She gave me clothes that apparently my father wouldn't allow her to have because of where they came from (she received clothes from her ex-husband's parents). Next thing I knew, I came home one day, and they were all gone. What?

My mother had given me a free phone home card, because in those days you had a home phone, you didn't have mobile phones. That was pretty much the extent of technology in those days. I had this free call to home, and my mum would pick up all the charges. But my dad was travelling so much that his wife was basically the ruler of me, and she wouldn't allow me to call my mum. I don't know what it was, but it was really upsetting for my mum and me. I never fully understood why she would not allow me to talk to my own mum. Whether it was the fact that she thought it was going to impact her phone bill, or whether she just didn't want me to tie up the lines. I never got told any of that, and you know, when you're dealing with a 15-year-old you sort of have to explain some things to them when making a rule. That's my take, anyways.

Chapter 3: Shattered Plans

One night, I had enough of her crap. My dad was away, and I packed up all my belongings into boxes and grabbed her car keys and legged it. I had no idea where to go, all I knew was I needed to get out and get away from her. She was cruel, and I couldn't take anymore. She came running up the street in her nightie after me. I couldn't believe it. I kept running, to the end of the street and further. I looked around, and finally she had stopped. I didn't – I ran a few blocks to someone in the church, and they drove me to another friend's place.

I got there and debriefed a little, and then a call came through. "Is Ria there?" What the hell? I was fuming. It was the pastor of the church. He already had a run down from her of what took place. I was being ordered to give her keys back.

There was no "Are you ok?", "Anything we can do?" Nope. I was the Rebel child that could do no right. Bang!

So, I made a deal with the Pastor to go and get my things and drop off her keys. I got back there, and what do you know? She had rifled through all my belongings once again, taking out what she deemed fit. Why, thank you. I really have no words for this woman.

When my Dad came home and found out I was gone, he was fuming. I thought, 'Tough shit, you miserable cow.' Anyways, he wanted me to come for lunch after Sunday church service. Oh, how I wanted to say no. But once again, I fell at the whims of my dad. "Yes, daddy."

Ultimate Relationship: Part 1

Off I went, I sat at his dinner table, and then she started. "So, Ria, how is living on your own? Paying your own bills? Cooking your own food?" Oh my God, she wouldn't stop. I did not bite into her crap. But the more she went on, the more I got angrier within. What was her problem, anyway? I was here first. I had been here for 16 bloody years and she just met my father this year. Oh, she made my blood boil. I sat and said not a word.

Then, my Dad looked at her and said, "Have you had quite enough?" My jaw hit the ground, my heart even skipped a beat. My dad really does love me, he just stuck up for me. She didn't say boo after that. I still did not come back.

At least until my lease ran out on my place with my friend. About nine months later, I asked Dad if I can move back in. We had a conversation, as things had changed. I had a boyfriend and a job. So, we had to negotiate. I had to get my own way to work, pay board, buy all my own personals (shampoo, tampons, etc), and I had a curfew. Fine. I was pissed off that my tiny little wage had to purchase all these things, but I did it. It was the way they went around it.

I couldn't catch a break. They just kept being unreasonable, and apparently, I was living up to that rebel status. Next it was curfew issues and lack of communication.

My dad gave me a curfew. My curfew was 11, but he told her my curfew was 10. I'd go out with my boyfriend, I'd come back at 10:30. I was doing all the right things by my father, I had to, that was how I worked, I had to be that perfect child. So, when I had her literally at the door waiting for me at 10:30 going,

Chapter 3: Shattered Plans

"Where the hell were you?" I said, "Excuse me, that's not what my dad said." Then my dad would never back me up. You can't just make a goddamn bloody rule and expect them to follow it if you're not going to explain the reasons for why or the how.

Then I would come home from work and there was no food that I wanted to eat. So, I bought my own with my own wage. I would buy soup items and make a soup up. Then she bloody ate it on me. So, I thought I would beat her at this game. Keep in mind she was the 'adult' and I added pepper to my soup. She hated pepper and I knew it, but she dobbed on me and Dad asked for me to keep the chilli out. Huh? No.

So, one day I thought I would be nice and order them/organize them. Her pantry cupboards were always messy. She got in from shopping whilst I stood in the kitchen, she opened the cupboards and put her outstretched arms in there and swished it all around. I couldn't do anything right.

Then I put a photo of my mum and dad on their wedding day up on my mirror in my room. It was my room, right? Wrong. Next thing I knew, I was being asked to take it down. I said no. They are my parents. Dad requested that I take it down. So, I cut the photo in half and placed each parent on either side of my mirror. Nope, still not good enough for this woman. Take it down.

Then she decided to take it up a notch. It was her cleaning day, it was her washing day, and so on. I had gotten home from work and was making a soup. She asked me to go clean my hair off the floor in the bathroom. I said "Yes, I will do shortly,"

Ultimate Relationship: Part 1

as my hands were covered in potato skins. Nope, this was not good enough. She demanded I do it right this moment. I was dumbfounded. She grabbed the handle on the pot and I looked at her, I thought, 'Are you kidding?'

I said to myself, 'Let's play, shall we?' I grabbed the other handle, it was almost full to the brim as I had added the water before she pulled the pot. OK, game on! So, I pulled back. We played tug of war and as she pulled back, yep; I let it go. She went flying back on the dining room floor with the pot of soup and all the vegetables on top. I looked at her and said, "Yes, I will go and clean my hair off the bathroom floor now. Thanks."

It just got better with time. She kept coming at me and I kept matching her.

Chapter 4: Being a member of a Church

Chapter 4: Being a member of a Church

During my church days, the need for belonging was my utmost priority. I guess growing up in my family with each of my parents and then leaving it for choices of my own was very hard – and it had nothing to do with them as well. I just had to make sure it is written in this book and this is very clear – it was all to do with my choices.

When I moved to Queensland, I didn't have anybody but my dad. I had met some of these people from the church through brief trips I made up to the Sunshine Coast when I was visiting dad from the age of 12 to 15, and I formed some friendships with these people, but they were like 2-4 times a year type friends. Pen-pals existed back then too, so some letters were exchanged.

As time went on, I formed some really good friendships. One of the girls I moved out with at a time when things didn't work out with my father at the age of 16. I was always able to rely and call upon these people when I was in need. I guess that put me in a very vulnerable position, because when I was in need they were always there, until I did something wrong. And when I did something wrong, then I was called upon for discipline, or they would talk amongst themselves until they found out the gossip. This was really a massive for me.

For example, I had a boyfriend, but we both had been sexually active prior to the relationship. It was nobody else's business at the end of the day what we did or how or where we did it. I don't need to disclose any of those details, but they found it

Ultimate Relationship: Part 1

very much their business because I was a church member, and they found it plausible to discipline me for such actions.

Here I am thinking, 'I'm 16, I'm living by myself, I am responsible for my own actions, my own body, and here are these people that believe that they can take my life into their hands and literally shape me into doing what they want me to do. Conform to whatever.'

This just made me so sick and so upset that I could have people that would literally break my trust and be so secretive, and yet they seem to have conscience in what they were doing in their own world.

I did have lots of good memories; I had all these great friendships, I enjoyed Bible study and sneaking notes to the guy next to me who would eventually become my husband. I enjoyed Youth Group and getting outdoors and having clean, wholesome fun. I enjoyed singing, but I was ridiculed for it. My voice wasn't as good as some of the others, this upset me. But I kept on singing. I loved many hymns once upon a time, and they would rock my world. I loved being around older generations and being able to chat to them and be their friend. I thoroughly enjoyed helping them wherever I could.

A dear old man whom I will never forget gave me a substantial engagement/wedding gift the day I got married because he was so grateful I took the time for him and said hello at every opportunity. Rest in Peace.

Chapter 4: Being a member of a Church

When they started to control my every move, it got to the point that I started to rebel against the teachings. Something in me was not agreeing anymore, and I chose to walk away. When I left the church I soon started to realize the amount of fear that they pumped down my throat and how they had brainwashed me. I couldn't see it whilst I was surrounded by it, but my eyes quickly opened once I was out, so to speak. I also noticed on an epic scale that all those people that I came to call my friends and family seemed to disappear. Not sure whether it was me that disappeared from them because I was the unremorseful sinner, or it was them that seemed to disappear when I left. One thing for sure was that this particular group was only there for you when you were a part of their pack. This was very sad to me on so many levels, because I truly treasured my friendships.

You can teach about love, but fear has nothing to do with love. It was their idea of controlling me, like to be told what music I could listen to, when music was my life. Music had the ability to pick me up out of dark places. Music was and has always been my solitude. Music has been just one of those go-to places, you know when you get hurt and you find that one piece and crank it up on high and feel it through your body. You let the music take you to a place where it is just you in your own paradise. Where you are safe, you are supported, and you let yourself go into the music.

My favourite songs that have withstood the test of time are:

Stand by Me – The Pretenders

Ultimate Relationship: Part 1

Killing me Softly – The Fugees

Pocketful of Sunshine & These Words – Natasha Bedingfield

I pick my choice of song, whatever comes to me at that time, and it just allows me to drop into the motion or the feeling of whatever it is at that time, whether I need to release or not. That's what I let it be. But, I had been told that my music was satanic, it was this and that, and I ended up believing all of that. I ended up doing this ritual – it is quite hilarious actually – the church condemned all these satanic rituals, yet here I was doing exactly that. At least, that's how it felt.

There I was one afternoon with my 12 CDs that I had, which was like Janet Jackson and Mariah Carey, and I smashed them with a hammer. Not to make me feel good, to make my dad feel good, and Michelle feel good. He said that I could go to the church, stand before them and say that I smashed all my CDs. Seriously, if that's not a satanic ritual, what the fuck is.

I only made them feel good, it didn't make me feel good, it didn't do anything for me in my morals and values. It's just one of those things, but I guess the crux of it for me was when they started to control my relationship when I was with my boyfriend.

Being in the church and looking for belonging was very strange for me because it provided that space of connection, friendship, and to me it was only short-lived because when you decide that you don't want to follow the church or their

Chapter 4: Being a member of a Church

rules then there is no connection, not from your behalf but from theirs.

Unfortunately, that doesn't sound like true friendship to me, just because it's somebody's choice not to go to a church. I don't believe they should be ostracized because of that, because friends don't do that to each other.

One of the pivotal moments for me was when I found out about how the pastor's wife had gone about finding some details about me. She went to one of my best friends and hounded her about my relationship with my boyfriend. I was 16 and he was 26. She literally just asked and asked questions; that pastor's wife had no right to actually ask questions, it was none of her business. She got what she needed and then the shaming started.

They can say that they're doing it out of love and care or whatever, but it doesn't always make it right. My journey is mine and mine alone. They had no jurisdiction on that. I didn't sign no contract within the church to say I have to follow their rules and do what they say. Arrgh, they made me angry when they said I'm not allowed to have a relationship with my partner. They knew nothing, they think that they knew because when you go and kneel near pastor's pew and ask for forgiveness, you shame yourself every single time. At least this is how I felt for many years afterwards.

They brought this knowledge to our attention; not that they even had to, but it certainly felt like they needed to. They called my boyfriend into the office as a matter of urgency,

Ultimate Relationship: Part 1

then they confronted him about our relations, our sexual relations, which is absolutely nobody's fucking business.

We then had conditions to follow and abide by – yes, we had conditions after that, following that meeting. That we're not allowed to go anywhere together as a couple without a chaperone, ever. Until we were married.

I couldn't think of anything more ludicrous in my life, but you know what, we ended up having someone follow us around everywhere we went for the remainder months of our engagement. Before we married. I guess this is nothing to some, but when you have a rule compounded by the whisperings of a church group. Oh yes, they all knew. They were all watching. They were waiting for me to fuck it up so they could dob on me and feel justified in the moment of their good deed. Oh, please. I couldn't think of anything more pathetic than waiting for someone to fall just so you can lift yourself up and get a false sense of joy, or whatever it is they felt by doing such acts.

After we married, I just got she shits with the church and said, "This is not for me." So, I started pulling away from the church. For myself, really, at that time, because I still stayed there physically but I think it just got me more and more frustrated. I guess I could say that I finally made my decision to leave the church when I was being told when to bring in morning tea, when to join the busy-bee and clean up the gardens, when I was on mowing duty. When I looked at the church newsletter, and I was on the duties list and they never even had basic

Chapter 4: Being a member of a Church

courtesy to ask if I would? I got a bee in my bonnet and walked away. You see, I used to cook every other week anyway and bring it to morning tea. I didn't do it for the thanks from anybody else, I just did it because I loved to do it. I love gardening and mowing too. But I will not be told to do things with love, and I absolutely detest people not asking. It's not how it works.

I felt such a loss when I left as there was a few times when I actually walked down the main street of town and I'd see people from the church that I thought loved me, I was part of the family, and now they wouldn't say a word to me. They didn't even look at me, they didn't even acknowledge me. I know that they saw me, but they wouldn't even acknowledge me because I was no longer part of the membership. It was really, really horrible. That's what ended my journey with the church. This affected me for many years to come.

Chapter 5: Married at Eighteen

Chapter 5: Married at Eighteen

I was engaged at 17 and married at 18. I don't know how many people told me, "Don't do it, don't do it, you're too young..." I was living out of home at this time, but this didn't stop people getting involved.

My dad had to sit down and have a meeting with my fiancé and me because he had to make sure I knew all the guidelines. What we were meant we had to have in place before we married. The list we needed was:

- Have our own car
- Have a deposit for a house
- Have $$$ in the bank
- Etc.

At the time I believed there was some truth to it, however I think the way it was delivered to me made my skin crawl. I just went, "Screw that shit, I am not listening". Yep, I chucked a tantrum, and I was going to do things my way. I am pretty sure he never had all those things when he married my mother.

Then my boyfriend had to have a meeting with the pastor and go over the hall, the marriage ceremony... I don't really know as I was never involved in these conversations. In that church there was only men-to-men talks because the men were the authority and my thoughts were that women didn't matter as we were always excluded. They talked about many things, these men, and us women just had to bow down and obey. I snickered to myself some days and thought, 'Yeah right, you haven't met me, have you?'

Ultimate Relationship: Part 1

Did I mention? I had no dancing, as this is not acceptable with the church. I had no alcohol, as it is the root of many evils. Even the music had to be accepted by the church, and we couldn't have anything mainstream or alternative, etc. This caused issues within itself. As I asked the church for some music that would be acceptable for my ceremony. I was given music to listen to, and then told that I can't choose that song as it was their song, etc. So many frustrations.

We got married in a Uniting Church, as the church I attended actually did not have a church building they could call their own. They met in a school building when I was attending.

I was nervous on the day, and barely heard a word about the ceremony. The marriage ceremony, I found out later, was the Pastor's opportunity to preach the gospel to my non-believing family members. They were not impressed. The reception took place in a hall. I had invited many of my family, despite the dynamics over the years, and when they accepted I was faced with a dilemma: I had to seat them in the same room together. I solved my problem and I put the food in the middle of the room and seated all chairs in a circle around the room. Giving them the ability to sit wherever and as far away from whoever if needed. Well, they all decided to sit next to each other. I got a life lesson this day, and that was not to try and please everyone, as it was so exhausting. I was very happy that it all went well, and whatever had gone on within the family they kept it to themselves and did not bring it to my wedding day.

Chapter 5: Married at Eighteen

I did, however, have a honeymoon, and it was there I believe I started to think I was crazy. I had this huge amount of guilt rush in for all the times that I slept with my boyfriend before I got married. All the times before this relationship that I had been footloose and reckless. I even thought that maybe I should go 18 months without sex to try and repair the damage. To get forgiveness for my wrong doing. Luckily, my new husband didn't think I was crazy, just that that was a crazy thought, and we had a great week on a secluded beach and did loads of shopping and window shopping. The blame and guilt did not go away, I just found a way to repress it, to shove it down so that I did not have to deal with it.

Married life started. It felt great to set up the house my way. We did it on a small budget. We found a cheap 2-bedroom rental for $115 a week. We accepted second hand furniture and collected household knick-knacks to furnish the house, and the church supplied us with a hamper of food to fill our cupboards, which was kind.

My husband was working for a company where he was asked to work away during the week. He had been doing this for couple of months by this time, but I just had this feeling that something was off. I asked him when he came back from one of these trips, was he doing something? I wasn't thinking cheating, but it is his story to tell, not mine. He couldn't look at me, nor could he say no. My heart sunk. I knew the answer to my question. I was gutted. I had been working three jobs round the clock to keep myself busy and occupied whilst he was away, and he was doing this?

Ultimate Relationship: Part 1

I found being lied to really difficult and hard to deal with. They didn't tell me this in the marriage counselling sessions. Oh, yeah, that's right, women were obsolete. I did take it really really hard, but he still continued to travel with work and continue what he was doing until the job was complete.

The next moment of significance was when I found out I was pregnant. He was still away at the time. I was ever so excited, and I managed to tell almost everybody I knew before I even got in touch with him, even though I tried countless times. I left him to call his family. I thought that was kind.

The pregnancy was progressing very well. At least, until I found out what I was having. This was a little hard to hide. My mother-in-law took me to the ultrasound because I wasn't driving the car at that stage. The doctor knew what the sex of the baby was. I was not too happy, as I did want a surprise. I said to the imaging consultant, "If you know what I'm going to have I need to know, as I can't have another person know and not me."

In that next moment, we found out I was having a little girl. I was gobsmacked. On my husband's side of the family tree, the only one girl born in five generations died in her early ages. At least, this is what I was told. I felt quite blessed and ecstatic to be having my own daughter. I felt grateful that I was able to have this little girl growing inside of me.

When I told my mother-in-law, she was ecstatic, she thought it was the best thing ever. But then I had one of those bittersweet moments, where I told my father-in-law, and holy

Chapter 5: Married at Eighteen

moly did he hit the roof. He's just like, "Oh my gosh, you know girls are so much trouble." This is a father of three boys telling me, a first-time mum, that girls are so much trouble because, clearly, he knew all there was to know about little girls. I really should just shut my mouth and never share my joy.

I then thought I would call my own father and tell him the news of my little girl. My husband's father had voiced his opinion. I wasn't too impressed. My father would be delighted, wouldn't he?

Um, no, I barely got through to him and shared my joy with him and whoa! The preaching started. "Well don't think I am going to be the babysitter." Don't this, don't that. I just crawled up on my seat and started sobbing. I could not believe my ears. My own father, why is he talking like this? I was gutted for days and did not speak to him for the remainder of my pregnancy.

During the pregnancy I had a moment that brought a smile to my dial. Thinking of all those people at the church that thought and spoke about my life. My thought was that I didn't fall pregnant for about 18 months after we married. So many people in the church thought that I was getting married because I was young and already pregnant, which was quite hilarious when I passed nine months of being married and no baby popped out.

Things started escalating as I had this new baby to think about. We felt we had to move from the three-bedroom unit into something bigger. The current living arrangements were in a

Ultimate Relationship: Part 1

unit with stairs, and I'm like, "I'm not going to be climbing up these stairs at nine months pregnant, so we've got to find a house." There I was, looking for a place.

We found a house and I had covered all the specifics with the real estate. At least, so I thought. I had explained that I was pregnant and that I wanted to set up and stay at least the year. The real estate had confirmed that this had been an investment property. This was great as everything seemed to fit. Until we moved in, at least. The minute we moved in we noticed an overkill of cockroaches in the home. The real estate said, "It's your problem." Then I started to tidy up the overgrown gardens and found all these keys. My thoughts started to go wild, wondering where all these keys went, who else had them. Paranoia set in. Meanwhile I developed a big dislike for cockroaches. I felt so dirty seeing all these cockroaches and I couldn't keep them away despite all my attempts.

We lived five doors down from my husband's parents, which I thought it was really good at the time. Learnt quickly how wrong I was. His dad and I had finally been getting along, saying hello when I walked in the door, and seriously that was an effort from him, as I'd spent the first 18 months of my relationship with my boyfriend/fiancé with his father not talking to me or acknowledging me. That was the best as I could hope for looking back, really.

If my father in law was calling us on the landline (the phone attached to the wall with a cord, haha) and he couldn't get in

Chapter 5: Married at Eighteen

touch with us, he would walk up the street and knock on the door, shout "get off the phone", walk back home and try calling again. I was miffed about it, but he had his ways.

I was always on the phone at this time and I had this list next to the phone of all the people in my life that I wanted to keep in contact with. Every single day I had a couple of people to call so that I could keep in touch with them all. I felt it was important that I kept in contact with all my family and friends on a regular basis, not just once every blue moon. It got to the point where I thought, 'Oh my God, this is freaking crazy.' I can't keep this up. I am seriously the only one that keeps calling. So, I just stopped calling everyone. Friendship is a two-way street, it is not always up to me.

After 5 months of making the house and everything ready for baby, we got news from the real estate that they wanted to sell the house. I was eight months pregnant, and I remember thinking, 'How am I going to be in this house when I'm about to drop a baby, and they up and sell it on me, and I have got to pack, I have got to plan, I'm going to have to move to the new house, unpack... it's just not going to happen.' I rang the real estate in a panic, but they said, "It's business." I didn't like it one bit, so I was like, "Ok, well, I am not going to stay here any longer, either."

I quickly jumped into action. I found another house and got approved. I had the house packed in three days, and there I was, two weeks later, running around and cleaning the house

Ultimate Relationship: Part 1

with this eight-month belly with sciatica shooting through my legs. The pain was excruciating, but I did not stop.

At one point I was on my knees wiping the skirting boards, and my knees would give way and there I was, laying on my baby. I was so glad to move into the new house, which was so much nicer. We got settled and I got to set up a room ready for my baby girl. I sewed her bedding for her cot. I made her curtains. I couldn't be happier.

I had my little girl, and it was like all the problems of my world disappeared. She definitely changed something in me. When I got home, I just went with the flow each day. She fed for like 45 minutes to an hour, I couldn't help but feel like a cow. When she woke through the night I would get a cup of tea, 2 pieces of toast with strawberry jam and watch a movie on Austar. I would be awake for the duration of the movie. I attended a mothers group that I walked to each week as I was not allowed to drive my husband's car. This was apparently because it was in his dad's name still.

Life went pretty smoothly. We purchased a block of land and went and found a house plan we liked. Our house started to be built. I was finally allowed to drive the car. Wow. I was so excited.

As our house was being built I would drive over to keep an eye on it. I trusted few people and I wanted to make sure they did things right. Seriously, who was I kidding? I was 21 years of age and what did I really know about building my house, or to actually know what was a fault? It didn't matter. I found faults

Chapter 5: Married at Eighteen

and I let the builder know. Picked up a couple of speeding fines on my trips from our rental to the new house.

When my daughter was 18 months old I went for a trip out to collect some Tupperware. But apparently, I was driving it to an area I wasn't allowed to, there was some limits on where I could drive into. I found this out when the engine started smoking. I pulled the car over to a safe place and I called my husband about 20 minutes from home with our baby, and he just yelled at me... "Can't believe you have driven out there, why did you go up there, I can't believe this." I was so upset.

I asked him if he was going to come and to see and collect us and he was like "No." And there I am on the side of the road abandoned with a little child. One of his best mates at that time happened to drive-by and saw his car, saying, "If she's still there I'll collect her." I was still there, of course, because I didn't know what I else to do. I had no awareness about what to do when the car breaks down, I was young and all I could think of was me and my baby. This friend of my husbands picked us up and drove us home. I was so grateful to him.

I was just so pissed when he got home, and I took myself to the mailbox. Oh, look at that, a letter from the transport department telling me I reached my quota of fine points from two speeding tickets as I was only on my provisional license. So lucky me: I had the option of taking a provisional point for a year or suspension for three months. Well that just topped me off. I decided to have a glass of white wine, and then another one, and then another one. I was just so fucking angry

Ultimate Relationship: Part 1

with him. A few days later I realised I was pregnant again. Although it took over six weeks to convince the doctors. Pee tests were negative, and it took two blood tests before my pregnancy hormone started to elevate to the point where the doctor could confirm I was pregnant. The pregnancy went so smoothly. I dry-reached for most of it as I did with my first pregnancy, and I learnt to eat what I was craving at that moment, whereas my first pregnancy I lived off 12 litres of milk a week (yep, by myself), fresh bread rolls and butter, and hot potato chips.

I got to full term and the doctors wanted me to wait until the 25th, but according to my dates he was already two weeks overdue. They asked me in for a routine check up on the 21st and found his heart rate low. So, they got us in to check again the next day. All was 100% and the hospital was quiet too. I asked if they could induce, me as they had reason for me to be there and I felt that it would be best to have him out.

Two hours later, after they followed protocols to check if this could happen, I was finally being induced. They sent my husband home and said it will take hours. He just got home and sat down with a cup of tea and they were calling him as I was in full blown labour. Shit was getting real. This was happening really fast. Three hours from cream to the birth of my son. When he was born he couldn't hold his temperature. They had to put him under heat lamps. I barely got to hold him over the next three days, and the nurses were all so conflicting with all their ridiculous ideas of motherhood and feeding. My son was in an incubator with sunglasses on, in a nappy after

Chapter 5: Married at Eighteen

nine months of being snug as a bug within me. They would tell he is not latching, I am not feeding him correctly. I needed out. My daughter was struggling with the whole concept of me not being at home. I got home, and I mothered my children the way I wanted to.

Six months on, Nash continued to grow and develop as children do, and my daughter was almost three, and they were really good kids.

As my son grew, he was such a good baby. He made lots of noise when he slept, but he was so quiet. Friends would come over and not even know he was in the room as he was so placid. I remember going to the doctor as I felt that something was going amiss with the feeding. My son fed so quickly compared to my daughter. The doctor ran some tests and my body was being drained of all nutrients. My son was clearly getting them all. However, I had to make a choice – and that was to continue feeding my son or stop so that I could nourish myself. I would provide bottles of formula for him. So, I chose to stop feeding my baby boy. This decision crippled me deep down. I had never felt so guilty and so much anguish for not being able to provide the 'best' foundation for my son.

However, I was struggling inside, I didn't think I was coping. I wasn't coping as well with this baby, or with being a mother of two children, as I did with being a mother of one child. But I didn't tell anybody, because god forbid, I couldn't tell anybody or they'd think, 'What kind of mother are you?' They already had big judgements; "You're a young mother, you're

Ultimate Relationship: Part 1

not handling this or that." I said fuck it, I will figure it out, and that's what I did. But it just got to the point when my husband would come home from work and I would walk out the door. I would place my son on the floor and I would walk out the door. "I've got to go have some time out." And he'd just look at me like, "What the fuck is happening today?" But I couldn't talk to him, I just couldn't find the words to explain what was going on inside. How can I tell somebody when I have no fucking clue what is going on? All I knew is that something was seriously fucked up inside of me, something was going on.

One day I felt so bad that I drove myself to the doctor with my two kids, I walked up to the desk and said, "I need to see my doctor." They said, "She's too busy today." I said, actually probably more like yelled and pointed, "That's ok. See that chair over there? I'm going to sit there and stay there until my doctor can see me, because if I go home today I don't know what is going to happen to me. I'm not placing any threats here, but I know that I need to see a doctor because if I don't, I don't know what tomorrow is going to look like."

I probably sat there for an hour and a half, and miraculously my doctor found some time for me. I wonder if the receptionist/s saw my desperation and actually squeezed me in.

I wonder how many others come for help and get turned away. You know, like that moment in the movie Dangerous Minds where the child in the classroom goes to get some help from the principal of the school but is rejected because he

Chapter 5: Married at Eighteen

didn't knock on the door or use his manners. Then, he went out and faced this trouble alone, and he got shot. And it happens time and time and time again in society. Lo and behold, I don't know what would have happened if my doctor didn't see me that day, who knows? Through universal power, through me wanting that help, somehow it was meant to happen.

So, the doctor asked me about 10 questions and then concluded, "Oh, you're not feeling too good, are you?"

Which I replied, "No, not really."

"You have post-natal depression."

I'm like… 'Oh, well that really makes me feel ten times better getting that diagnosis… NOT.' This just made me feel like more of failure. My head just spun with all the thoughts of how I failed…

Lastly, the doctor prescribed me anti-depressants and recommended I see a counsellor.

I went home and wondered how on earth I could tell my husband. Not sure when this took place, but he wasn't impressed. I should have told him, he said.

Just when I thought it couldn't get any harder. We were in the lounge and my son was playing in his jungle gym on the floor, but his face was going bright red and I was just like, "What the hell is happening? He's not breathing!"

Ultimate Relationship: Part 1

Off to the doctor again, it was a weekend and we got in to see the doctor on duty. Holy moly, I was ever so grateful for his doctor, even though I didn't like what she said. I went in and told her about how my son was on all fours crawling, playing on the carpet and his face was bright red like he couldn't breathe, and she goes, "What colour was his face?" I said, "It was red, he was struggling." And she said, "Don't worry about that, if it's blue that's when you got to worry because when it's blue there's no oxygen going to his brain; at least when it's red there's oxygen going to his brain."

I'm like, for fucks sake, do you doctors ever listen to how you actually communicate to a parent? Could you not have said that in a better way? They could've found some empathy and said, "You know what, as really concerning as that was for you, just so you know if it ever happens again, fingers crossed it doesn't, that you don't have to worry so much because there is actually oxygen going through his brain." That would've made me feel ten times better than the way that they made me feel.

Anyways, this doctor worked marvellously in getting me to see a paediatrician. They said, "You might be waiting a while." Within two weeks we got to see a paediatrician. We were then given another referral to a specialist at the children's hospital, which was apparently gonna be another long wait; however, within three weeks we were in to see the specialist. Next thing I knew, was my son was having tests to find out what was wrong, and he had to go under and I had to watch him go under; I just had stay tough. I just had to stay strong.

Chapter 5: Married at Eighteen

We got our answer – my son had Tracheomalacia and Laryngomalacia. This meant that his airways were a third of the size of what they should have been at his age, and also his larynx was blocking his airways. So much to learn, and I find out that many children are simply diagnosed with asthma instead. My son was given steroid treatment when he was unwell to open his airways. So, my little boy had a diagnosis and treatment. He just kept going, and hospitals became a part of our lives. We got quite acquainted with the specialists and the play rooms.

Chapter 6: Marriage Not Going to Plan

Chapter 6: Marriage Not Going to Plan

I continued to take my son to every specialist appointment and learn more each visit. However, we got to about 18 months old and he barely spoke. My daughter had a 50-word vocabulary at six months old, and I talk a lot. So, back for more tests. He also didn't eat solid food – he would just suck it dry and not swallow it. He wouldn't chew it, he would just spit it out. We still couldn't work out why he wasn't eating food, so more tests, more tests, and more trips to the hospital. We did a test for swallowing liquids and solids, and there was nothing wrong with his swallowing capacity. It wasn't until they did another test where they found out that his tongue only moved in and out, it didn't move side to side.

It's nothing major. It only moved in and out. This meant he couldn't swallow, he couldn't chew because the tongue wasn't moving in ways that the brain registered. This also meant that he couldn't talk.

We went to a speech pathologist and they gave me some exercises to develop and change this. They simply told us to put finger food in bite-sized pieces at the sides of his mouth and it would literally send signals to his brain to go, "Hey tongue, you can go over to your cheek and pull the food out and chew it." It was the most miraculous thing. In just 24 hours he was chewing food, he was starting to talk. I am sure he knew the words inside but just couldn't actually vocalize them until now because of the lack of movement with his tongue.

Ultimate Relationship: Part 1

From then on, there was no stopping him. He continued to grow and develop, and never seemed bothered by these issues, despite the many trips to doctors and specialists.

The time flew by with all these appointments. I personally didn't feel any better, I just had many distractions over the years to keep me from dealing with my own issues. And so, I went back to work. I became a waitress in my favourite Mexican restaurant. More diversion, I felt like I could breathe again.

I would get the kids bathed and ready for bed and have dinner cooked by 5.20pm every night. My husband said that he was lonely when I went to work. So, I taught him online chatting. You know, MSN Messenger (the days before Facebook and Myspace). This became his social outlet, and then he ventured into online chat rooms on his own. I thought it was all good. I would tell myself that when I came home I could look over his shoulder and see what he was writing. Which I did, until this one night I got home late and found him talking to this chick. It wasn't that he was talking to a chick that was a problem – it was the content. He had mentioned his needs not being met, and she was replying with, "Just part the red sea and go for it." I hit the roof. I pushed my husband aside and went to town on this COW. I was fuming.

When my son started to go to childcare and my daughter was at school, I volunteered in her school tuckshop and later got a job there. I also got a job at the local IGA.

Chapter 6: Marriage Not Going to Plan

I kept finding things to keep myself busy. I felt like the marriage wasn't going anywhere. There are many other reasons for why, but as they involve another person, I have kept them private. I did feel at one point that he had no respect for me and my role as his wife and the mother of his children. This really became my governing thought. You see, I went and bought things for him and drove to pick up things for him. I just got to a point where this is not what I wanted to do. This is not what I wanted to go down for in life.

With everything going on inside of me I felt the need to sit down and ask my husband, "Well, do you still love me?" and the answer I heard was 'No, I do not love you anymore. You're not the same person.' I was just gutted.

I had to go through the motions of that and contemplate what that meant for me. Basically, over the next nine months I contemplated that thought, I talked about it with my friends as most people do, not just most females. Nine months later I just said, "That's enough, I don't want this anymore. I am ending this." He was gutted, as I had been for the last nine months dealing with someone (or dealing with the contemplation of someone) that didn't love me. When that happened, I just threw everything into a spin. At first, I felt really good that I actually made the decision to step up; that I just decided for myself and actually followed through with it. However, sometimes we do not think things through or contemplate the consequences of our actions.

Ultimate Relationship: Part 1

We split in February 2009 as I had made the decision to end our relationship and marriage. I saw nothing wrong with going out and having some drinks with friends. I suddenly felt so free. That weekend I even kissed another man.

However, as I found out. My husband did not seem to understand it when I said I don't want this anymore and it's over. I guess he didn't see it this way. So, when he found out that I kissed another man, he found this as betrayal and made sure that his family and friends knew that I had cheated on him. Well at least, that's the story that I got.

After 13 years, my family and friends were also his family and vice versa, and he had been telling them how much he loved me, and how much he wanted to be back with me, yet five weeks later he's met someone and he's with somebody in a relationship.

This shattered me on so many levels. I know I made the choice to leave. I know all of these things. But this also shifted something within me; like, 'What have you done?' All this doubt over whether I made the right decision. You look into your kids' eyes and you see the pain of your decision in their eyes. It cuts deep into your core. The living situation was made worse of course, as we were still living under the same roof. This went on for seven months after I decided to split with him. I wanted him to move out and he wouldn't move out. I tried to move out, but I didn't have a job that earned as much as his. No one wanted to take me on.

Chapter 6: Marriage Not Going to Plan

This arrangement became difficult because here I was living under the same roof with the same person I just split up with after 13 years. Him having a girlfriend, me getting the kids to school, go to work, him going to work.

By night, I couldn't bear to be in this home anymore. The more I stayed the more my chest felt like it was going to explode. So, I needed relief and did what I did best: drink and let loose like no one cares.

Now, as I am looking back on it it's just so bizarre as it's something I would never do it again. I learned lots and lots of lessons from that. I guess for me it was just like I was going out every night; Tuesday to Sunday, hanging out with my friends, only I couldn't be in the house when he was home. So, I went out, got drunk, blotto, whatever, that's what I had to do with the time. At the same time, I remember my thought being that I just felt so empowered within myself in so many ways because I was always able to be myself in whatever way that that brought me. I felt stronger within myself, I felt so much more confident. People were saying that I was always being reckless, that I needed to slow down, but... you know, without telling me how, don't tell me. Because those kinds of comments just fall on deaf ears.

I was going out most nights, working two jobs through the days. Tuckshop 8-2 and then IGA 2.30 till close. Then I would go out in the evenings. The kids were safe with their father. However, drinking as many nights as I did, sleeping, or the lack

Ultimate Relationship: Part 1

thereof, was catching up with me. The week prior to me leaving to the States was not my finest.

By Monday before I left, I found myself crying to a dear friend wanting it to stop! Wanting life to stop! I was trying to think of ways to make it stop! The pain inside was so intense, I could not keep on like this. Unknown to me on the Saturday night before I went to the USA, I was drugged! I had only a couple of wines with a friend, and then I was found leaving the club with a girl and guy I had never met. My girlfriend was told I was staying at the Mantra, so she believed I was safe. This was so not the case. As I woke in a house in the back of some suburbia area. I rolled over to see what time it was – 6:00am. I sat up as there was a male and female in the bed. At this point what had gone on did not disturb me (yet) as I was concerned with getting my belongings. I was in this room with two people and I was like, "Where are my things?" Another person from another room brought them to me in someone's hat. Then I said, "Where are my clothes?" I had to walk into another room for those. Still so unperturbed about what actually went on. I just needed to get home.

I finally got back home and called my girlfriend and said come get me at my work. I had just gone in and got some credit. However, due to my state I had forgotten to pay for it and the staff were laughing at how crap I looked (shrugs).

The next day I was called into work a shift at the tuckshop. Well that day was not great, let me tell you. My boss was off and I had volunteers around me, and this school admin person

Chapter 6: Marriage Not Going to Plan

had come down and told me that I'm not allowed to open up my mouth and I'm not allowed to speak bad, and I just went, "Excuse me? Who do you think you are?" I took her into the store room and said, "You will not tell me what to do because I am doing my job, it's as simple as that. I'm doing my job, so you can go back and sit on your chair and do the work you need to do, not come down here and do stuff that's not in your job description."

Anyways, this was reported, and I was put on probation for four days. Then I left there for the day and I went into my work at the IGA and was told that I'd stolen something. I sat and watched the footage and just looked with disbelief. What could I say. It was most certainly not intentional. I offered to pay immediately for my $10 credit. Oh, and there was also an issue with the video rentals, as I was told by senior staff that they just took videos and watched them without paying for them. Me being me, I scanned them through the system and reduced the cost, to have a trail of who had what. So, this just amped their case against me and I was without a job. I wasn't sacked but just informed there would no longer be any hours for me.

I sat and cried to my girlfriend in the carpark. Cried and cried. Wanting it all to stop. She asked me to drive to her and we could talk. I really didn't think that was a good idea. It wasn't. You see, as I drove and cried, I thought of all the ways that I could stop this pain that I was feeling. I thought of ways I could run my car off the road, hit this telegraph pole or the next one. Or spin my car off the road to hit a ditch. I was thinking

Ultimate Relationship: Part 1

thoughts like if I could just hit that tree then the impact would hopefully take away the pain that I was currently in.

With all these thoughts, I knew that whatever I did do, I couldn't break my legs. I needed to walk on the plane in 5 days. Before I knew it, I was at my friend's place. Hardest drive I ever took.

Anyway, in May, things had gotten pretty hectic, and basically, I was offered a trip to go to the USA for some time out with my Aunty. The details get a bit foggy for me here and all I know was that my sister and my aunties sorted it out. $900 return ticket to LA, then a short flight to Arizona and my aunty was going to take me to Vegas whilst I was there.

On my flight over there, I was sitting next to this Canadian fellow. We got talking and there were some delays on the meals so we just said to the staff to keep bringing drinks to us. Well, the first one I thought they mixed before serving. Umm, no. We just threw down straight gin and we were well on our way. We got cosy talking about movies and one thing led to another, and we found our way in through the gates of the Mile-High Club. We got sprung by the staff and they did warn us that none of that should go on. We were so cut by this time that we laughed and chuckled to ourselves as they couldn't exactly kick us off the plane. Anyway, we snuggled up with a blanket, told the staff we had just gotten married and slept the rest of the trip.

I absolutely had a ball over in the states, and I was ever so grateful for my auntie and my sister for the opportunity. One

Chapter 6: Marriage Not Going to Plan

evening I was out at this posh club in Scottsdale and thought I would call home and talk to my kids. My daughter so excited to hear me, but also was very excited to tell me of Daddies girlfriend too. I went from 0 to 100 and was totally in the 'What the fuck?' space!

I got her father on the phone and reminded him of our arrangement which was that I did not wish him to introduce his girlfriend to the kids whilst I was not in the country and she was not to come to the home. This was my wish whilst I was gone, and it might have been unreasonable to others, but to me, this is all I asked. This conversation did not end well. He tried to explain, "She just stopped in on her way to Netball with her kids." I did the time zone calculation. It was a Saturday at 7am in Australia. I wasn't having any of it. Gosh, my kids had found so much out in a short time for someone that has just stopped in on their way to Netball. Oh, my head spun. Ended the phone call. Went to the bar.

In Scottsdale, when you ask for a drink they free pour. I was ordering vodka shots and vodka & orange juices. So, as I drank I sparked up a conversation that with this friendly chick at the bar. After a few hours I went to the toilet, which were so large that they had a make-up artist and a nail artist inside the amenity block. I thought it was quite hilarious, and I had a lovely chat with her, probably drunk as a skunk, but she was really really lovely.

Next thing I knew I was wrapped around the toilet bowl, and the chick from the bar found me and told me my uncle was

Ultimate Relationship: Part 1

looking for me. She also made me aware that there is zero tolerance for drunkenness. I had to wait whilst she talked to the security and informed them that I was a tourist and my uncle was here to take me home. This would keep me out without any trouble. I said to security, "I'm not going to give you any trouble, I just need to go home."

My uncle came and found me because my auntie had already left a few hours earlier and he stood around to keep an eye on me. The girl I met at the bar brought me out and my uncle got on the other side of me and helped her carry me out. Although I actually didn't make it more than about five steps out of the toilet block and found a bin on the post and puked in that on the way out. We got out of the bar quickly and my uncle didn't let me get into a cab until I sobered up a little bit, so we did a few laps walking around Scottsdale until I stopped throwing up. Then, we hopped into a cab, and oh my God I was feeling the urge to be sick again. The cab driver was amazing, he goes, "Just open up the door and do it out the door, outside the car".

So, there I am in the middle of Scottsdale, the door open, and just puking. I left a little charming remark on Scottsdale when I was there. Sorry people of Scottsdale, but I did actually enjoy my time there, until I made myself rotten drunk.

I then went on this amazing bus tour up into the Grand Canyon. The tour lady was so fluid with her knowledge of the Canyon. The deaths, the live animals and all the stories. Plus, all the people on the bus were just amazing.

Chapter 6: Marriage Not Going to Plan

Then I had my trip to Vegas. Oh, they say "What happens in Vegas stays in Vegas." We stayed in the Egyptian Resort/hotel. I found the whole experience amazing. It opened my eyes but at the same time opened my mind as what we are shown in Australia is so different to the actual experience. I found it one of the safest places that I had ever drunk alcohol, and I danced the night away with strangers that became friends by the end of the evening.

One of my experiences was when this amazing singer on stage left his post to sing on the bar, where a girl got up and body danced with him. Then he stopped in the midst of his set and said he was taking a break for 45 minutes and took off with this chick. So funny. Only in Vegas.

Being on the other side of the world brought a lot of home truths home for me. What was real? What was important? What did I want from life? Etc.

Then, on one of the last few days I was there my dear friend called me. He made my heart swell in that phone call. He knows who he is, and I will truly be grateful for his friendship and support over the years, and especially in those months leading up to my trip. He is one in a million, and I will always love him.

When I was flying back home there was the swine flu going around Australia. When I'd left Australia, there were only three cases of it, however on the flight back from the States I found out this had turned quickly into a massive outbreak.

Ultimate Relationship: Part 1

I contacted my child's father in regard to me coming back there, and he said "No, you can't come back to the house because you could have swine flu." This meant I couldn't go to work and the kids couldn't go to school.

I don't know, I just could not believe that I was being refused... it felt to me I was being refused entry into my own home, to see my own children. At the end of the day, we are all screened on a heat screen when we got off the plane, and there was actually a couple of people that were taken in because they'd come up on the heat screen and registered as having some form of swine flu, I guess. But this was not me.

Anyhow, I'm sitting in Brisbane, balling my eyes out not knowing what to do. I called one of my aunties and was saying, "I don't know what to do, I can't go home, I don't have anywhere to go, I'm out of money because I just came back from the States, I planned on coming home straight away." That was not the case. I did have a bus to go to, but I wasn't able to go home. My aunty (thank you), she bought a night at the Mantra in Mooloolaba for me, and I stayed the night there, which was really good. I met with a couple of friends and we went out for a bit. I had an early night as I was jetlagged.

The weekend passed, and then on the Monday I booked myself into the doctor. I got nose swabbed, which was one of the most disgusting, vulgar things I've ever had ever to go through in so many ways. I was dry reaching, I was gagging. It was vile. Got me tested, got it all clear. I got the results within hours due to it being urgent so that I could get back to work.

Chapter 6: Marriage Not Going to Plan

So that Monday afternoon I walked into the school grounds with my letter and my head held high, and I got to see the look on my kids' eyes when they saw me. I was so glad to see them, I was so ecstatic. I thought about telling work that I could work the next day and I just went 'Nah, they can go fuck themselves.' They didn't have the jurisdiction to keep me away. They knew when I would be back. I've done all the tests, and I passed at the very get-go and they were just being ridiculous fear mongering idiots. Anyway, that was my frame of mind at that time.

I guess I had a lot of realizations being over there and being away from so many people I loved and cared for. When I got back, or when I was over there and coming back, I don't know where about it was – I realized how reckless I was being. I still went out. I wasn't going out just to get my rocks off or get blotto. I just went out, enjoyed myself with my girls and had some fun times. I got back in June, and for June, July, August, September, that's how it was. Though I was still sort of following that road, it wasn't as bad.

When I met with my girls when I got back, I was given some information that made so much sense to me about that screwed up weekend, and everything came flooding back. And not to justify my actions, but I found out when me and my friend had a glass of wine around 10, we had both been drugged. She had also found herself in a strange environment, and not a pretty one. If I'd knew more about it, if I had more awareness, it would've been a very different story. However,

Ultimate Relationship: Part 1

I'd probably have been down in the police station rather than going in to my work and not paying for my $10.00 credit.

When I got back things slowed down for me. I started to get my head back together in as many ways as I possibly could at the time. I finally found a place to live, I was so excited to get out of this home that was fucking with my head. By October, I was meeting someone on a blind date, and not in the most conventional way. We were set up through my girlfriend as it was her cousin. There was to be absolutely no attachment, no relationship, neither of us wanted that, we just adult relations and none of the club bullshit.

Except that's not how the plan went, once again my plan just kept on freaking not going to plan because I really liked him, and he really liked me as it turned out. We just hit it off from the get-go. We spent lots and lots of time together, our kids shared time together. We weren't admitting that we were happy, just spending time together without any need to put a label on it.

Chapter 7: Self-Sabotage in its Finest Form

Chapter 7: Self-Sabotage in its Finest Form

When I met this guy, we had this instant connection. It was certainly more than either of us were expecting on our blind date. During us meeting up and introducing our children over the next three months, he also got some insight into my lovely family. I mean that with a lot of love. I was living with my sister and her best friend at the time, and pretty sure my baby brother was staying there also at some stage.

My sister worked at night, so did her best friend. They were in the hospitality industry. We were all in a place of just letting loose, it was the first sort of place that we had on our own, I was sort of coming to terms with everything slowly, and finally I guess getting on a straight and narrow. Settling myself down after months and months of drinking and… well, I had some extremely fun moments, and some not-so-fun moments. At the time, it was bloody brilliant.

When I met this guy, he would come over to my place on most nights but go home by midnight. My sister and her friend would have the Mondays and Tuesdays off as they are the quietest nights in the industry.

We had our music playing but not that loud, as we could hear each other over the volume. We would be drinking, and one thing led to another, I was getting noise complaints because apparently our neighbours didn't like us. We'd just be generally talking, we wouldn't play our music really loud, it was more of the fact that we used to sit outside and chat and laugh, but apparently some people don't like hearing other people's laughter, giggling, etc. Each to their own, lessons

Ultimate Relationship: Part 1

were learned... Basically, I'd been coming up to the end of my lease and one weekend I stayed over at my guy's place. My sister also did not stay at the home which left my baby brother to my place and he thought it would be fun to get into my alcohol and have a few mates around. My house was trashed.

I had one of the biggest complaints from the real estate regarding noise. He wasn't even meant to be living there. Anyhow, I spoke to the real estate about it and basically not signing another lease was my only option. However, this left me with no references and in need of a home. I could've moved in with the guy I was seeing, but that wasn't going to work too well because he was living with his cousin, and she was going out with my ex-husband... crazy, crazy times. It just kind of happened like that.

I asked my ex-husband, "I need to move back into the house because I have got nowhere else to go." There was a massive shift between three houses, so the guy I was seeing actually moved in with me into my old house with the children. My sister, her friend and my other brother were also staying there. So, I had, I don't know, maybe 5-6 adults in there, plus 4 kids. My ex-husband moved into the house with my guy's cousin.

That was really sort of crazy, crazy, crazy times. It was working, having basically my two brothers living with me, my sisters living with me, her friend living with me, four kids literally all shucked up in one little laundry room, but yeah, I was clearly not in the best state. We sort of worked with it as much as we

Chapter 7: Self-Sabotage in its Finest Form

possibly could, but there were just too many people... bills weren't being paid, I was forking out $400.00 a week on food, contributions weren't getting paid so there was a lot of animosity.

Fights started to happen. The cops landed on our doorstep one night because I had a massive argument with my brother, not my baby brother but the one just down from me. There was a lot of yelling going on, and I just poured myself a glass of vodka with lemonade and tried to walk outside to go and have a smoke. As I walked past him, he started on me again and I was like, "Fuck you, here's my glass of vodka!" and I threw it all over him, I hadn't touched a drop.

I went back to the kitchen because I was even more pissed off then as I had just thrown my drink all over him and had to go pour myself another one. I hadn't realized the drink I just threw at him was also all over the floor, so I ended up slipping on it, and I came crashing down on my hip as my legs disappeared from under me and I had hit my head and my elbow on the home gym, and I screamed bloody murder.

My partner came running into the room and thought that my brother had done something to me. He came out and said, "What did you do?" My brother said "nothing" and stormed off outside the house. Next thing I know, the police were at the door. Really, what for? I was still so angry from the argument that I just had with my brother, and then the police were like, "We've had a domestic violence complaint about this address from a neighbour." and I'm like, "??? I beg your

Ultimate Relationship: Part 1

pardon, there hasn't been any violence here." and the police said, "Are you the only one here?" and I replied, "No, I'm not the only one here, I got my siblings here, I got my kids inside, etc".

Anyway, they police were trying to say that they heard that somebody was slammed up against the glass window and I'm like "Well that just didn't happen". The police apparently didn't like me telling them what had actually happened, they weren't listening to me. They said they have been to many homes where this occurs, and they don't believe me. Arrrgghhh.

Anyway, I was just in full aggression mode then because I'm just like, "How dare you tell me I've been violated in a domestic violence altercation when that hasn't even happened?" I had told them I fell after yelling at my brother, but he had not touched me. I had the second drink that I had just poured in my hand. They asked if it was alcohol, which I replied yes but I hadn't had any yet. They didn't believe that comment either, but they didn't breathalyse me for proof. They were questioning my partner, and then they just kept on at me and at me, and I just... I had to wonder why they even bothered sometimes, because here I am, nothing has happened, they're trying to tell me something did, yet there are other people getting bashed up. It was just a really, really nasty night. But one thing led to another because I wouldn't shut my mouth – my partner had to pull me aside and tell me to shut my mouth because the police where threatening the paddy wagon.

Chapter 7: Self-Sabotage in its Finest Form

Then, they had asked to speak to one of us in front of the garage. They looked inside my sister's car, which was off the road on my property, and they saw a road sign in there. At the end of the day, I'm not responsible for my sister's actions, or her friend's actions, so then they asked to talk to my sister. They said it was illegal for that to happen, and then they put my sister in the back of the paddy wagon.

You know how to get someone's goat when they already got their goat and then your pull it harder. I tell you; I just was like nuts. So, they checked up my license while they had my sister in the paddy wagon, and they found some offenses linked to my name. Unbeknownst to them, I was actually almost at the end of the 18-month battle with the court because there was a case of mistaken identity and a girl had used my ID while I was in the United States to go out illegally while she was underage.

She had committed some offenses and told them her name – Ria Nicholls (my name). These were not pretty offences either – they were urinating and being drunk in public places. The police again where not believing me, and this as you can just imagine just infuriated me even more. They had my sister in the paddy wagon, then they try to tell me that I'm not such a saint because I got these offenses on my name, which was not the truth because I was actually out of the country when they took place. The police were not listening to me, and they let my sister go. So, nothing took place except for the police squabbling with us about what is and what isn't. End of the night.

Ultimate Relationship: Part 1

I did, however, get them wiped thanks to the great help of a judge at the court house and my proof of being out of the country, which I'm ever so grateful for.

It was around January or February when I moved back into my family home where I raised my children. March came, and it was my sister's birthday. I had a party and, once again, the cops got called because we had some music playing, not so loud, but apparently too loud for some of my neighbours. We were all talking and hearing ourselves over the music, however it seemed to loud for our neighbours. Party poopers, I say. Police came down to tell us to turn it down otherwise they'd confiscate the speakers. So, we all resorted to our mobile phones and had no further house calls from the police. Phones aren't too loud, and we had a reasonably good night.

The next day I woke up and I felt like I was getting an allergic reaction; my legs were swollen, and I had this rash all up my legs. I still went to work as per what I do, I just push through and keep going, but I was getting pain through my body and I had to leave work, it was just ridiculous. Basically, the pain just got worse, worse and worse, and I had to go to the doctor and get checked up for what I thought was this allergy. I didn't know what I ate that could have made me think it was an allergy.

This pain just seared throughout my body, and the doctor knew I was in some significant pain, and he prescribed me some painkillers, and they worked for a little bit. After a couple of weeks, the pain just got gradually worse. It was just turned

Chapter 7: Self-Sabotage in its Finest Form

into a constant battle to ease the pain because I didn't know any other way to get rid of the pain. The doctor finally took some bloods because he started to suspect it was Ross River because of the significant pain that I was in, and he prescribed some stronger painkillers. When you get Ross River virus from a mosquito you need to sleep and rest, and rest, and sleep, but that was not an option for me. I did not do that, I had two children to provide for so that's what I did. Meanwhile, the pain was obviously going to get worse because I wasn't resting, I wasn't giving my body the time to recover from this virus that one fucking little mosquito came and gave me. I think it took about six weeks for the bloods to get back and for it to finally come back positive with Ross River virus.

By that stage I was put on a painkiller called Tramal and Tramadol, which is a synthetic opioid drug originally made with the intention of not being addictive (let's call it morphine for the sake of my book), and I had no idea what it was. I just knew it was a painkiller and it was bloody working. Before I knew it, I was on slow release tablets and instant release tablets, and unbeknownst to me I was addicted before I found out what the drug was.

I could feel this fight going on inside of my body because I was now, in my head (and believe me, there's a lot of fucked up crazy shit that goes up in my head), the junkie, because I knew without a doubt I was addicted to it.

You can imagine when things are already at peaking point with your family. Things weren't going so well, it was just crippling

Ultimate Relationship: Part 1

moment after crippling moment. Basically, it got to a point where my partner had taken me and the children away to the Gold Coast for a weekend getaway. He took me away to get me some rest as well as for the kids' sake.

I was getting phone calls from my siblings and their boyfriends or their girlfriends and asking me this and that, I was just like "Shut the fuck up, let me have some fucking space!" and it just didn't stop.

One of the last phone calls I had, well, basically one of my siblings or their friends wanted to get into my room for whatever bloody reason and my partner and I had locked the door. We locked it because a brand-new hard drive got stolen out of our room.

I had questioned everybody, and apparently nobody took it... So, I did what I knew best and investigated the situation. I called every pawn shop in the area and where potential locations could have been privy to my belongings. What do you know? It was sold to a pawn shop in the time period that it disappeared from my location. As apparently no one took it from my home, it somehow walked its way all the way to Caboolture (40 min drive away) and got sold in a pawn shop in Caboolture. I knew it was mine because somebody that I knew (lived with even) worked across the road and they had access to that bedroom.

Whatever, it was done, it was dusted, but I locked my room and they wanted to get in to get the vacuum. Like seriously, they weren't doing anything (meaning they were not

Chapter 7: Self-Sabotage in its Finest Form

contributing to the household) prior to me going away, so what the fuck are they going to do while I'm gone for one weekend?

My head was in crazy-shit mode, and then I got a phone call from my brother's friend, and he was telling me he was going to commit suicide and blah blah blah, and I was like "Seriously? I'm just done with this shit, go and do it if that's what you want." I was so at my own end of my own rope, and yeah, I said things.

It may have not been the right thing to say, but I said it. Then I had my sister calling me up because that was such a horrible thing to say to somebody. Yeah, I get it. Anyhow, we got back on the Sunday night and they were all gone, my siblings were gone, they moved out except for one of my brothers.

When they all moved out I just felt absolutely guttered, broken. I don't really know why, because I was so grateful that they had gone because it was so much pressure off me at that time. I knew things weren't right with me, but I couldn't make it right. I just did not know how, everyone was just like, "Do this, do that," but it's not so easy when you got a body filled with pain and you know you have to take those painkillers to rid yourself of that pain.

Months went by and a lot of Facebook slander happened between us all. Friends of either side of the fence felt like they needed to contribute. Contribute to bullshit. I felt so like my heart was ripped up by all of them, really. I also felt really bad for my children because that was their family, and they moved

Ultimate Relationship: Part 1

out and they didn't say goodbye. There was just so many emotions that were coming up inside of me, and I couldn't explain them. Like, when I sat there with my kids and they're like, "Are we going to see such-and-such again?" and I didn't know what to say to them. There was a lot of gut wrenching moments there.

One of my self-sabotage moments was before I actually moved into the house, when I was living with my sisters (they were born to my father from a different mother, but they're still my blood). One of the family members on their mum's side had passed and I wanted to go to the funeral as support for my sister; however, I was told that I was not welcome. That really crushed me because I just didn't know why, I had not done anything wrong towards that family, I don't understand why they would stop me from being a support. Maybe that was not what they were trying to do at all, but in my head that's exactly what it felt like. That night I was really reeling, and the pain inside of me, my chest was freaking caneing and I took a whole tray of a painkillers. Yes, the heavy duty Tramal ones. It was not the best moment in my life, but it stopped the pain, it stopped the fucking pain. It made me very numb.

I went back to the bedroom and I told my boyfriend that I had taken all these tablets. Looking back, it was probably one of the cruellest things you can do to somebody. If I didn't tell him he'd probably would have slept better, but that night he didn't sleep a wink because he had his hand on my heart the whole night waiting for my heart to stop because I just gone and overdosed on tablets (not for the first time – through high

Chapter 7: Self-Sabotage in its Finest Form

school years I took trays of Panadol, trays of Nurofen, you know, just to numb the pain, and it did that, it did exactly that). I knew that the tablets were my go to for me, I guess because they're easy to take. I don't believe I had any intention of suicide at that time, but I tell you what, I fucking wanted that pain to stop and if you read suicide stories that's exactly what they want to stop, they want that pain to stop.

Anyway, I lived, obviously, to tell this story. Going back to when my family had just moved out, obviously things went from worst to worst to worst, and I don't know what's worse than worse but it just kept on... it was just like a spiral, I was just in a spiral going down, sinking, sinking and sinking and it didn't really matter what I tried to do to get myself out of it, I just kept on going down the sinkhole.

It sounds really strange, but I really love mowing the lawns. Why I love mowing the lawns – I love the instant satisfaction. I know it sounds like I'm a bit off track here, but with having all these tablets and having this addiction, being stuck in this moment in time where I wanted to NOT be addicted, but I had to take them because the pain was so severe, but when do I KNOW when I'm not in pain to not take them because I'm on them all the time. So, there was definitely this inner chaotic crap going on within me.

It was difficult, but I couldn't explain to anybody back then, I couldn't really make sense of it because – and so many people will be so please for me to say the words – I wasn't acting out of a rational space because you can't, you just can't. I was

Ultimate Relationship: Part 1

acting in flight-or-fight mode, and pretty much had been my whole entire life.

Basically, I just finished mowing the lawn, I was getting quite sick of the postman (this will sound really crazy) riding his bike over my beautifully manicured lawns, so I tied a rope up from the council tree to the letter box. Unbeknownst to me, that's apparently illegal... I had no mail or something and so I called up the post and I yelled at them. This was my thing, yell at whoever is fucking with me. It wasn't so many nice words either, but I did it.

Next thing I know, the post contractor was at my house with the mailman and I was like, "What the hell is going on?" I walked out there and I just let loose, and I had this massive fight with the postman and the post contractor. It wasn't a pretty sight. I ended up coming inside and I couldn't breathe, and my chest was pounding like so fast and heavy, it was like my heart was literally going to bust out of my chest. I thought it was going to explode, and I couldn't breathe.

My brother was just like, "What the fuck is going on?" and I was like, "I don't know, I can't breathe, I can't breathe, this is so fucked up I don't know what to do!" and he's like, "I'll take you to the hospital." and I said, "I think I need to go to hospital, I can't breathe, something is going on with my heart" and he said, "I'm taking you to the hospital." and I said "No."

I didn't accept help from anybody.

Chapter 7: Self-Sabotage in its Finest Form

So, I grabbed all my tablets, all my morphine, all my anti-inflammatories, I grabbed everything. I think I was on anti-inflammatory, fluid retention, slow-released morphine, instantaneous morphine... I was a concoction of freaking tablets, and I filled the brown paper bag with them all, and drove myself to the hospital (how I made there safely I don't know, but I did) and I walked into the emergency ward up to the nurse station you have to go and I threw them at the nurse and said "Get these things away from me, they are fucking me up, they're fucking my life up!" I don't know what was wrong and I was just losing it, and as I write this I am funnily enough getting quite emotional.

Probably because it was a such hard time in my life and honest to God it was so hard to be addicted to something and not know how to get away from it, not know how to get out of it. So, as I cry and continue to write my life down in words ...

Next thing I know, I'm being seen to by a psychologist because I've just literally had a mental breakdown and I was on a considerable number of tablets, probably more than I should've been, and I stood there begging the nurses: "I need those tablets, I need them!" Which I did, I was still in pain.

Then, I had to go to the doctor every two days to get my tablets because he had to administer them into two-day lots because I was on watch because I lost my shit, I lost it in a big way. It was probably one of the safest things I did do. At the end of the day, somebody was keeping an eye on me and how many tablets I was taking, and if I took all of them in those two

Ultimate Relationship: Part 1

days then I couldn't take anymore, so I had to really find some self-control within myself and just take what the prescribed amount was.

A couple of months later, I was at work and I was getting a lot of pain around my kidney area. This addiction to morphine was four and a half months long. I probably don't remember a lot of the events that happened that time because clearly morphine fogs the mind, creates paranoia. I was at work, and I told the manager in charge that night that I needed to leave work, that I was in a lot of pain, and they wouldn't let me go. I drove home after work and told my partner, "I gotta go to the hospital, I'm in a considerable amount of pain." I went to the hospital I told them this is where the pain is. They ended up putting me on Endone. I stayed overnight, I was pretty freaked out, but they put me on Endone and for whatever reason, I can't even remember if they found anything, I don't really think they really would've, but that was my it, that was my moment.

When I was discharged to go home, they gave me a prescription of Endone... I had it at the hospital, but after that moment I didn't need any of the tablets for whatever reason. I didn't have any of the pain anymore, it was like gone. Or maybe there was no more pain? Maybe it was all in my head after the addiction took over?

Maybe it's quite a different story for everybody else, but of my memory lapses of that moment, of that time, that's all I have.

Chapter 7: Self-Sabotage in its Finest Form

I left my job at the end of the year because I heard some stuff go on; I just didn't think it was appropriate to be talking like that without making a formal complaint against the person they were talking about. I basically was the whistle blower, and I blew the whistle on a situation that was going down at work. One of my colleagues had left and it was about them, and things got a hell of a lot tougher for me at work. I just found it very hard to work at work. I turned up to my shifts and they would change my shifts and tell me, "Sorry, your shift doesn't start for another three hours." They were rostering me on days that I had been approved to have off. I put a few comments on Facebook without mentioning names or businesses and not even who, or what it was involving. Like, "Is part time meant to regular hours?", "I am sick of this bullshit." Really, nothing personal or detrimental. However, it seemed that a few of my colleagues that I had added to my Facebook felt that my comments could be given to the boss to 'sink' me.

So, one weekday, I was going to a Bon Jovi concert with my boyfriend, which I was so looking forward to, and I had a call from work saying that I've got a HR complaint against me, and I need to go for a HR meeting in the morning and that I could bring a support person. It just wasn't pretty. I went to my meeting, I brought a support person. Thank you, you know who you are. I said not a thing, I did not agree with their complaint. Man, I was so proud of myself. I went in there and they were hoping I would blow off the handle and lose my shit so they could sack me. Haha, I got news for them, I stayed.

Ultimate Relationship: Part 1

So, for whatever reasons they had, I really did not want to work with people that treated their staff the way they did. A few days before Christmas, the busiest time of the year I quit, I quit my job. I made my stand and would not take shit like that. I acted professional.

I had one of the most relaxing Christmas ever, it was really quite nice. I didn't leave them in the best situation, but sometimes you have to do what you have to do for your own health, and that seriously was a benefit to my own health to get out of there.

I started inquiring about doing some family day care, and in January of the following year I got accepted. I set up my home and started a day care in February-March, and by April I had a booking, and then in May one of the other local educators had to stop her family day care suddenly, so all of her bookings came over to me and all of a sudden, I was fully booked. I loved it, I loved doing my family day care. But I signed into too many hours too fast, and meanwhile, I was running my business from home, I was working 5am-7pm 6 days a week.

I decided to start proceedings with my ex-husband and divorce him, so I did that. Another lesson learned: don't freaking divorce until you do your settlement, because you only have a year after you divorce to settle property. At least, this was what I was told. If this happens to you, get your property and custody sorted first, and then divorce. I learned that the hard way, as most things – I did my divorce and then I did my settlement/custody. We had lots of discussions in cafes and

Chapter 7: Self-Sabotage in its Finest Form

public places, but we came to an arrangement that we agreed on. I chose public places, I chose them for so many reasons. There were cameras if things got out of hand. There were people around, so the conversation stayed civil. It was a neutral area. No partners around to add their input, no kids of ours to be distracted with.

But there was lots of drinking, why-nots and arguments. Anyway, that whole story is going to be in another book, just leave that one where it is.

Chapter 8: Running Away

Chapter 8: Running Away

I left that job and, in my mind, I was going to not work for anybody, and I decided that I would do my day-care. I inquired into it, and I got refused because apparently there wasn't a big ask in my area. I then proceeded to just do some research, get to literally believe that I was going to start my day-care. I had a beautiful Christmas with no work and all that jazz, but I needed something to pay the bills. I ended up getting accepted by Scheme to do my day-care.

It was the same Scheme that rejected me before, and I questioned them as to why they would refuse me, because at the end of the day it's a self-employed business. I just needed to run underneath their name and then I would be up and running. With that conversation under my belt; I did a few of their basic courses and I had myself up and running. I got my first booking in March, I was so excited. It was just once for a fortnight on a Saturday, and I didn't really want to work Saturdays, but you know what, it was a booking, take it. So that's what I did.

Sort of went against my grain there, compared to what I know now, which literally started off that rig moral; it's not like I was putting the wrong foot forward, but as I made that decision to work when I didn't want to work, everything else sort of coincided with it, as it always does.

I started this booking and about three or four weeks later I got a call from Scheme saying one of the other ladies in the area had to stop for personal reasons, and I was like "Oh, that's awful," and then I happened to get all of her full bookings.

Ultimate Relationship: Part 1

That was really, really nice, so I pretty much went from one booking, which was an all-day fortnightly Saturday (they were great kids) and basically went into full time Monday to Friday. I threw myself in further and further, week to week, so I was doing 8 to 5, but then as time progressed through the year there were a few spots here and there and the time I was working went from 8 to 5 to 7 to 5, to 6 to 5, to 6 to 6... and I got some bookings that wanted before-school, which was fine, really good, you just get them ready for school, or sometimes are already ready for school.

I remember this one lady who said she would be there at 6, she was paying from 6 o'clock in the morning to drop off and I take her kids to school; however, she would turn up at 5:30am, and clearly, she wasn't paying for that time before she her booking started. So, I would make sure the gates were locked, the doors were locked, and she couldn't get in, and I don't know what was going through her head because she wasn't paying for my services until 6 o'clock and I wasn't opening up my door until 6 o'clock.

I locked the doors, and unbeknownst to me this woman somehow got through the gate, I mustn't have locked that one, and she was knocking on the door, knocking on my back door, knocking on my laundry screen door (which rattles) and at 5:30 in the morning, then she went around the front and proceeded to ring my doorbell and wake the whole god damn house up. That just pissed me right off. For some reason or another I had, to some degree, been enabling that behaviour

Chapter 8: Running Away

– now, when I look back, I realise I'd gone against the grain and I'd taken work at times when I didn't want to.

Then I got some work from this lady, she was a young mum, she had three children that I was aware of, and the oldest one wouldn't be older than 6 or 7. She was a beautiful little girl, but quite unclean looking, and these 2 children, they were just like... so beautiful, but they didn't make a noise, they didn't cry, and I'm just like 'I got to get them into my care to give them an opportunity.' I just knew that I needed to get them into my care. Anyhow, she wasn't paying her bill. Luckily, they were obviously getting some part of the bill because when she signed them in and sign them out I was able to claim the CCB for her; however, she wasn't paying her out-of-pocket part. I believe I got her on to the jet payment through Centrelink and everything like that, which meant she had to pay less, but still she wasn't paying it. I had a waitlist of a couple of people that either wanted extra days and I just sort of had to start to look around and realize what the hell was going on with my business, because here I was ready to take on new bookings for the new year and yet I was looking after children for people who were not willing to pay for my services.

The first year went pretty swell, but I was not providing food. The second year I decided I was going to provide all food in my service because at the end of the day I wasn't happy to pull it out from the lunch boxes and giving them to these children because there was nothing more than junk in my eyes. I'm a true believer that what you put in is gonna cost you one way or another. You either put good food into your body to give

Ultimate Relationship: Part 1

you good health, or you pay for it later in the hospital with medical issues. At the end of the day, I don't mean it to come off harsh, but I think it's a lack of education... like I know it's out there, but I do believe generational habits through families, and the food getting predominately worse like packeted food and all that, like the wheat for instance – it's just not good quality wheat these days for many reasons – but that's not the point of my story. I also believed, tried and tested that huge amounts of sugar, colours, preservatives, etc. doesn't need to be there. You can have beautiful meals, beautiful snacks without any of that, and it also contributes to children's behaviour and God knows all the other health problems that are there just ready to be awakened by the shit food that's going into their bodies.

The following year I got all the approvals, follow the book as I do, and started providing my own meals. I obviously put up my prices, but I found meals that are easily made within my service on a day-to-day basis. It was the best thing ever, I had the children eating it all, eating things that they'd never eaten before at home, the families were stoked, they wanted to know how I got them to eat certain foods because they had tried it at home... there's obviously a few tricks around that as well, and I don't mean like trickery, but I just mean when you do it in a certain environment, with every single child eating it, and yourself eating it, there is that encouragement behind you. Routine and consistency also assist greatly.

But when you're in your own home, a lot of people they make comments like, "I can't believe I'm putting up this with this."

Chapter 8: Running Away

They don't understand the power of those words when you say, "Oh that's disgusting" or "That looks disgusting" or turn your nose up. Their children are watching and listening to every single comment that a parent makes, and if you happen to say it, they've heard it, and they will not try that food, whatsoever. Yet, they'll come to mine and they'll eat it at my day-care services.

That was really good, providing the food in my service was brilliant, and it just did so much for all of their little bodies. I know this sounds gross, but seriously when you're changing 30-odd nappies a day, you find a new appreciation for good food: when you can put a good food into a child, you have the children's body start to work in a very normal habitual way rather than these white pasty poos that look like white... you know, really I will probably make people go off rice custard or rice pudding, but that's just literally what they looked like. You can have a child literally not absorbing any food that was being provided by the parent, and that child could sit there all day long and just shit, shit, shit the whole time. I had this little girl, she got to the point where she was just eating three meals a day, she wasn't asking for anything more, she didn't need anything more, her nappies were of regular consistency, there was just so many aspects health wise that were so beneficial to these children.

Once again, I pushed myself to the limits. I worked the longer hours, doing the extra food; I was not working just five days of the week, I was working six days of the week because I took up some extra work on the other Saturdays, some Saturdays

Ultimate Relationship: Part 1

I'd be looking after 7 kids plus my own… my partner was there, and he was able to take our four children out. It just was taking its toll on me and I could feel myself whinging and bitching on a constant basis regarding situations: parents not paying, not getting that appreciation, etc. I got to the end of my tether basically, and it broke me. The new year started, and I was just struggling.

At the time I wasn't aware, I was calling up Scheme, I was telling them of certain situations with the children that I needed assistance with. I wasn't actually aware that someone could step in for me so that I could have an hour out if I needed, or just to have that support. When I found out about this support, I found it too late by then, and I really reached my threshold so when the children had their sleep I'd start to make some research, make some phone calls about what my options could be.

I looked into age care work, and about three months later I decided to pack it up. I packed up my day-care, I sold everything off. I gave four weeks for the families to find other places, which was good, most of them had found places in two weeks. After those two weeks was done, I started doing my age care course, three days a week and I loved it. I got my work placement, and I absolutely loved that. I went from one end spectrum to the other; however, I thought that I was leaving all those problems behind because I shut the doors of my day-care… that didn't happen. I just found them in a new environment, new people, new forms of shitty assholes really… so many aspects I realize now that I didn't then.

Chapter 8: Running Away

So, I went into age care. I started the age care in 2013, did my course, I think that's when I finished up my day-care, then went straight into age care. Did my course in eight or nine weeks, something ridiculous. One thing I've learnt is that when you show up and put in the effort, the shit gets done. You don't have to think about the end product all the time, you just need to show up and get it done.

So, what happened with that was I got my placement, got my job out of it, and then one of the other girls I did my placement with found a job elsewhere. It was good, I absolutely loved the work, I think it would have to be one of the most rewarding jobs I'd ever, ever done in my whole entire life. To be able to hold someone's hand before they pass, or to hold someone hands in those last fleeting moments where they could possibly be scared. Just to hold their hand and comfort them in their times of need when their family can't be there for whatever reasons, it taught me so much in that industry.

It taught me how beautiful the elderly are, not that I didn't know that before, but I guess we have so much to learn from them if we gave them the time instead of pushing them into these homes and throwing away the key because I believe that's what society is doing, especially in Australia. I know in other parts of the world they are integrating the age care, the elderly, the disabled, with other people, which they fundamentally need to do across the world. I learned how many issues that was within the industry as well because the food was not nutritious, and the medication had to compensate for the fact that the food was shit, and they had

Ultimate Relationship: Part 1

to have more medication to compensate the medication they were taking for the food being shit, and this vicious circle that these clients, these people were stuck in, and they had no voice.

They say that there are advocates out there, but there are not enough of them. That would be an amazing business to get up and running, and you know, to see every single elderly person actually be able to have an advocate on their side rather than these systems that are working against families on a day-to-day basis. I really have got to stop myself because I'm just going to get into a massive passion right there with that. I will leave that one for another story.

I learned loads of stuff there, it was very rewarding. However, once again, I was a casual. I could work as many hours as they saw fit, morning, day, night... and I was doing it. I had really not learned the word NO. Whenever they said YES, I jumped. I just did the amount of shifts I had to do, and there was a situation that was going on at work.

Let's backtrack. At the beginning of 2013 my partner and I actually decided we would go exercising for whatever reason, God knows what was going through our heads. We would go for a run, we had the dogs with us... I just finished calling to my children, "Watch out for the pine needles, they're very slippery."

Be careful what you wish for, be careful what you put out into the universe, because holy moly did it come back and bite me instantaneously. The moment that those words left my

Chapter 8: Running Away

mouth, I jumped off the road onto the foot path and my foot got stuck behind that tree root sticking out of the ground. My other foot slipped on the pine needles, and I bet you all are thinking the same thing, and you could see it happening a mile away, very predictable. I went through the air, and not only did I body-slam the pavement, but I did it right beside a bus stop on a busy suburban street. There I am, face-planted and screaming because holy moly, it hurt. I was 84 kilos at that time. My son was ahead of me; my daughter was behind me and she came bolting up to me, shit scared. My partner was trying to pick me up and I was like, "Don't touch me!" because while I'm lying there face down on the pavement I could hear this bus coming down the road, and I knew that there was going to be people on it because at the time of day that it was. And I was like, 'No way am I going to be picked up off the ground while that bus is right there because they probably saw the whole thing." So, I just waited until the bus had gone, then I could get up.

I didn't even contemplate any pain or anything like that.

I'm really finding interesting how scattered my mind is around this time of my life because it just went from bad to worse. Anyway, he picked me up and we went back to running home… I end up grazing both my knees, my elbows, and felt a little bit winded, as you do when you body-slam the pavement. Anyway, I ended up running. I walked halfway home from where I was, which is probably about maybe 750 meters, maybe 1k. I walked half that and then I ran half of the way, and then I went, "No, I'll just keep on going, it's all good."

Ultimate Relationship: Part 1

I was still doing the day-care at that time, picking up babies and God... I was lying there in the morning or night and I was just like, "It hurts to breathe." I was really struggling to lay on my back at night to sleep, and one of my parents worked in radiology and x-ray and stuff and I was telling her about and she said, "I think you should go get that checked out." This is four days later when I talked her about it, or maybe I told her about it through the week.

I went and got it checked out on the Friday, had the x-ray, obviously had to wait for the results from the doctor, you know how it is, you go get your x-ray then you have got to go back to the doctor, pay for another session, and then you get your results.

Why they just can't give you the results in the first place?

I did my x-ray and I gave it to her to have a look at, and sure enough I had actually fractured two of my ribs straight through, my L7 and L6, or my 6th and 7th rib on my right-hand side. I was quite chuffed with myself, to be honest, because it was the first time in my life I had broken a bone, and I couldn't freaking do anything about it. I remember thinking to a degree that at the only time that I actually do break my bone I actually can't get anything done with it, just my luck really.

I still continued with working, I didn't take any painkillers at that time because I resented any kind of painkillers, I refused to take them. But to be honest, I didn't even need them. The only thing I was focused on any point was one of my knees because it had a big graze on it. But that was pretty much it.

Chapter 8: Running Away

I was pretty chuffed with the fact that here I was actually breaking two of my ribs and I didn't even need painkillers, didn't even know I actually broke them for 4-5 days. My doctor knew that I didn't take anything because he knew my situation with the painkillers prior to this all happening, and he's just like, "My gosh, some grown men need a pethidine shot when things like that happen." But here I was... maybe my pain threshold was just so strong at that point, I don't know. Now let's go forward a little bit.

When I quit my day-care, I was doing my age care work, my studies, and that was about April.

In April I went and laid down because I had some horrid pain going on inside of me. I couldn't pinpoint where it was, and I was just in so much pain, but I refused these painkillers massively, I was like, "Nope, nope, nope, nope."

As I refused painkillers the pain got worse, and I'm telling my boyfriend, "I've got to call a doctor." It was like I just crashed. The doctor came over, ran some tests, I could not move. I was in absolute agony. I don't know if they forced me to go to a doctor or take a blood test or whether they just did it there, I can't honestly remember, but they were testing me for ovarian cysts and a baby in the fallopian tube. They were also testing me for bowel cancer, and I was just like "What?!" then I really started to think, 'Oh, utopic pregnancy.' Then I was just like, obviously when you get those kinds of suspicions your head just goes nuts, and mine was like tripping off its trolley.

Ultimate Relationship: Part 1

That was start of a 9-month journey of pain and suffering and fear, literally the fear was... to describe it now, that was the start of the fear awakening in my body to a degree that I know I wouldn't ever go back to, and even going back and trying to remember now is pretty interesting because there's a lot of blank spots there.

Through that nine months, I got told by the doctor that I was a "quandary". I had test after test after test; I had MRIs, x-rays, CT scans. The pain was in my lower area, like my abdomen area. The pain was just so crippling, and I had been convinced by a doctor to go on some anti-inflammatory meds because I was refusing the painkillers. I was happy with that decision, but it didn't make the pain any better. So, I could be walking around at work and next thing I would just cripple over a bench, and the pain is just intolerable, it just takes my breath away.

I take a few deep breaths, keep going back to my work. The pain in my back and abdomen area was almost like I was pregnant again, and I had sciatica in my back because when the pain struck it would cripple me, it would literally make my knees crumble underneath me. I had numbness in my leg, I was going to the toilet constantly, like... oh my gosh.

It's interesting now, writing it all down... it sounds bizarre, but I take a lot of joy in actually going to the toilet and taking a proper shit. But at that time, my bowels were so loose or whatever, anything that went in my mouth just came straight out, there wasn't anything to hold it in.

Chapter 8: Running Away

I went to the doctor and did all these tests; like they checked, they checked my bloods when I first came down in April with the pain, and the inflammatory level in my body... I think it's about 7-15 that your CRP level is meant to be sitting at (I think it's CRP), except that mine was 115. When the doctor saw that, she goes, "You shouldn't even be walking with that amount of pain, with your inflammatory level sitting at that high." There were probably other people out there that had higher results, but at the end of the day this was about me, my threshold, what I could handle, whether or not I was mentally handling it. I really don't think I was; however, to some degree I was physically handling because I was still taking no painkillers, I was just breathing through it and doing what I could do at the time. I do remember, though, that there was a part of me that... my paranoia started to build, my fear of food actually really started to kick in because it didn't matter what I ate, and you know, doing night shift to day shift, and swapping backwards and forwards. I think I was doing some ridiculous hours, 40 hours a week with my aged care, and they found me to be quite a responsible worker, and obviously I loved the people that I worked with and the clients.

I remember that this fear of food... I definitely wouldn't have called it a "fear of food" back then, but I was really freaking out about eating anything because it didn't really matter what I ate it was still going through me. My safe zone became my home-cooked food because if I went out there was this aspect of myself starting to believe that every single person was poisoning me. I know it sounds flipping crazy, but when you

Ultimate Relationship: Part 1

don't know what's going on, the doctors can't give you answers, and you know your body is having a reaction to something, especially when it's food... it would be straight through me within like 20 minutes.

I knew that there was food going into my body, and my body reacting with it somehow. I was a really good eater, I was eating curries, not all the time, like I was having slow-cooked stews and stuff. I cut back on my caramel lattes, which before then I would have 7 them of day – jumbo size, caramel shot, caramel syrup on top of that. So, I was making changes to what I was putting into me, and I had pretty much resorted to not eating anything through the day, or if I did I'd get one of those little V8 juice poppers just to get me that boost of energy because there was no point in really eating anything because anything I tried to put in my body I'd just throw it out the other end.

When you go through it day after day after day, it really starts to wear you thin. I was put on a waitlist for nine months. The urgent waitlist is what I got put on, to have a colonoscopy and – I can never say the word – endoscopy. It just didn't seem to ever come about. Meanwhile, the doctor couldn't find anything, or she could say, "I can see that you're in pain, but you're a quandary and I have no answer for you." Every one of my tests came back clear, even my CRP level dropped to somewhat normal, about the 30-40 range. Clearly there was still inflammation in my body because I was still in chronic amounts of pain, however. It may have considerably dropped, but it was that time in my life that when my pain was so

Chapter 8: Running Away

chronic it fucked up my thinking to the enth degree... there was just no way of saying that subtly.

I'm sure my mum would have some beautiful nice words. You only knew what you knew, or I don't know. I'm not trying to be sarcastic, mum, if you read this book, but I'm sure there was a lot of people that had really kind words at that time. But at the end of the day the pain was so severe, I was in full scared mode, I knew something was going on in my body but I couldn't work it out, and I was freaking scared of eating food.

December 2013 I was still working through it all: taking my kids to school, living my life, having friends over. I had paid for my grandparents to come visit us and spend Christmas with us. Doing anything to live my life as normal as possible regardless of the pain, and I think the busier I made it, to some degree, the more I took my mind off it; but that's all it did, take my mind off it momentarily.

About December 10th, just after my grandparents had arrived, I received a letter in the mail to state that my appointment for my day surgery was on the following week.

I remember being so pissed off because after waiting for so long I felt it was extremely inconvenient of the hospital to finally book me in when I had plans for my grandparents to come over and have Christmas with them. Anyway, I went in there and I'm not the best patient, I'm quite aware of that. I was pretty exhausted, I wasn't really sleeping much, I had bouts of insomnia that whole nine months and all that kind of

Ultimate Relationship: Part 1

stuff, and then I was having to take these horrible drinks two days prior to the day surgery.

When I got in there, I had to wait in the dressing gown, had to go lie on the bed, get the paper panties and gown on. The minute I laid down I fell asleep. When I woke up, I questioned the doctors about when we were going in, and they were like, "Well, you've already gone in." I was like, "No I haven't, no." They said, "Yes you have, but we can take you in again, if you want." I was like, "Oh, no." I was quite shocked that it all already happened: they had put the canular in as preparation for the investigations, so just after that is when I went to sleep myself. So, rather than waking me, as they already had my consent, they just ran the anaesthetic through the canular and proceeded to do the investigations.

I was sitting there thinking, "Oh my God, my hair isn't done!" I had one of those things on my finger and I kept knocking it off and setting the alarm bells off, and it was pissing off the nurses. Then I was like, "Well, I just want some food, can I have some food?" And they would say, "Yes, yes, yes." And then they'd get busy and forget me. They said I wasn't allowed to drive home and I had to get picked up. So, I got picked up and I wasn't allowed to do anything for like, I don't know, 48 hours.

When I got home, I sat outside, and, well, I can see that the lawn needs to be mowed and I wanted to go mow them. I was in my stubborn mode where I need to do these things otherwise they just don't get done. Basically, my grandfather

Chapter 8: Running Away

ended up going down and mowing the lawn for me, such a darling sweetheart he is.

Then, I think it was about a week later, just days before Christmas, after my grandparents had gone. The diagnosis had come in and it was evident that there were three holes burning on my small intestine – I had Crohns. I'd sort of known what that was, I read up on a few things because obviously they came to a number of conclusions and suspicions about what it was but nothing concrete. When the results came in, even though I'd read up a little bit about it, it still shocked the pants off me.

I started thinking about all the things related to this diagnosis, and my head was spinning so fast that I couldn't really make a hell of a lot of sense out of it all, but Christmas was all gone, and I was back to work. I had to work Christmas Day, which I was not impressed about. I started making phone calls to family regarding my superannuation, my life insurance, etc. just making sure that they would know where it all is and that they'd look after my children, or at least my family could see them if they were in their dad's full care. I was reading anything and everything on Crohns, filling my head with the worst-case scenarios about what Crohns does to your body.

The more I read, the more I saw that there was no quality of life to Crohns, and I would, as the years went on, literally just get more and more of my bowel cut out until I ended up with a bowel bag.

Ultimate Relationship: Part 1

From working in the aged care industry, I knew what I believed to be quality of life, and this diagnosis to me was not that. There was no quality in having a life with that kind of disorder. So, in that moment, obviously I made my phone calls. There was so much stuff, and I did follow through with it all, but I started contemplating where I was and what was going on. For whatever reason, I was thinking that if I moved away, that somehow it would get better, it would get easier.

Then, a defining moment for me was what happened next. My partner had come home one morning from picking up his boys, he went out with them – maybe it was afternoon, honest to God my memory is so shocking for that period of time. Anyhow, he just walked in and he was so quiet. He had been up all night feeling sick because he thought he had food poisoning, we'd had a take away dinner. I was in major shut down mode at that time, like I was just focusing on reading things on my phone, I was smoking, I was drinking, I was just in total "fuck you, world" mode because of what was going on for me, both known and unknown at the time, but I knew something was not 100%.

I said to him that day, "I think you better go to the hospital, because something is wrong." He was in pain. We took him down to the hospital – sure enough, his appendix had burst, and he had to wait for an ambulance and then get transferred. He was supposed to go in for surgery that night, but they just injected him with more morphine and antibiotics to stop the toxins poisoning his body.

Chapter 8: Running Away

The next morning, he had his surgery, and I was still working my shifts at work; it was overwhelming, so I ended up getting my cousin to call up my work for me, as I struggled so much with letting people down. I found it so much easier to ask someone else to call and cancel my shifts on my behalf. It was too hard – I just remember feeling, 'I can't work; this is all going on and I can't function with my own health, let alone his health, and trying to work on top of all that.' As it was still the holidays, my kids were over with their father, so that was a massive saving grace for me.

We waited until we got the call that he was out of surgery because it was only supposed to be a short one; however, it went for four hours, I think, and they literally wheeled him out of the surgery straight into the ward because it had taken so long to clean up the massive mess from the appendix bursting.

When I saw him, looking back now and being able to make sense of what I was actually thinking and seeing at that time, it was almost like seeing my reflection right there. I'm not trying to take away from his moment of empathy or anything like that, but the minute that I saw him he had tubes coming out of him all over his body and I had to turn away... (tears) He wasn't meant to look like that, he was just meant to have a few holes, a few cuts, keyhole surgery, and it was just meant to be a quick surgery, and it just wasn't.

Yes, I'm crying now, because that was so much at the time, and I guess the tears are also there because I know what I did after that. We left him to rest because he was coming off the

Ultimate Relationship: Part 1

drugs and was pretty out of it from the surgery. We came back that afternoon and he was looking heaps better, stuff like that; however, the next morning I got a call from his sister that I had to get up there fast, something had gone wrong. I got up there and all of his organs had shut down due to the poisoning of his appendix bursting, he had to get another tube put in.

I just remember thinking like, 'This is too much to see, this is so difficult...' In retrospect, it was like I was seeing my reflection on the outside because of what was going on inside of me.

I sat there with him, day after day, I was up there three times a day – visiting him, then going home to let him rest, and coming back again. We were sitting there deciding on... you know, where we wanted to live, all that kind of stuff. Meanwhile, there was this flipside of me that was thinking of moving away and trying to make sense of what was going on for me, and I just couldn't really explain it. I didn't say anything to him because it was just not a good time, clearly.

I also put in to place court proceedings with my real estate agent because we'd been in there since about July or something and the house was an old house, and we had a rat infestation, and a mice infestation, we had massive amounts of inconveniences from tradies coming in and getting our house up to scratch. This was by now what I had expected from taking on a lease. I'm sure that this had a lot to do with my paranoia getting worse and everything else; I'm not trying to blame it, but it certainly contributed to my behaviours. I

Chapter 8: Running Away

believed that the house was un-liveable, and I'd had that thought from almost the very beginning and everything roller-coasted into a massive tornado. I'd been asking since November to get out of the lease, but the real estate did not even acknowledge me or my concerns. When he was in hospital, he told me he didn't want me to do this, but I did it anyway: I put a court proceeding in place so that I could leave the lease.

I felt that they had done the wrong thing. So, I got a letter in the post a couple of days after my boyfriend was out of hospital, and I had to go to court. My partner's dad came along with me. I got my wish to move out, except that they weren't going to pay any attention to the fact that our circumstances at the time that I moved in had significantly gone downhill. So, I was just like, "Oh my God…"

Now I had two weeks to pack up and move all of our belongings with my body in so much pain. He was unable to move, stretch or lift due to risking further complications to his surgery. I was so screwed, and it everything was just spinning, it was ever so difficult.

I had a talk to my boyfriend about my thoughts and what I was thinking of doing as we had to move anyways. He had come out of the hospital, and there I was telling him I was going to leave Queensland and go to Sydney to spend some time with family for some time out.

Well, I was so ill, but without any doubt in my mind I didn't want to leave him, that was not an option, and he knew that.

Ultimate Relationship: Part 1

However, things didn't play out as once again I had expected, when I moved down to Sydney he ended up breaking up with me about 2 days later, and I just lost it.

I just literally turned into a dysfunctional mess. I didn't walk.

I didn't go anywhere without my sunglasses on my head, inside or outside the house.

I felt like it was so difficult for me to do the everyday things, like going grocery shopping.

I tried to enrol my children in a school down there.

I just felt so out of control to the point of almost no return and I had gone over to my cousins a few times in that week… she knew I was in a pretty bad way.

Anyway, we went down beside the Hawkesbury river and we just sat there and watched the water. A lot of moments with no words. I was crying, and asking, "What the fuck?" and all these kinds of things. I said to her, "I can't keep going on like this, I've got to do something," so we talked about my options, and one of the options in my mind was to admit myself into a hospital and go into a padded ward because I was clearly not right in the head; however, I thought that they would medicate me and I did not want to be medicated, that was an absolute NO-NO for me. During my 10 years of being on antidepressants, I really believed that they just made the problems worse to be honest, because they numb all your feelings, they not only just numb the bad feelings, but also the

Chapter 8: Running Away

good ones, so you literally walk out like a zombie, something that's dead. I felt dead.

Nah, I draw the line with the medication sort of things, and not knowing about anything else I asked, "What am I going to do, what am I going to do?" So, we both started looking on the internet with our phones sitting in front of us, looking at retreats. I didn't know what they were, but I was just looking for somewhere where I could go and rest, somewhere they'd be able to help me out with my depression that I had been diagnosed a number of times over the last ten years. I had thought that this was my problem.

I contemplated just packing my life into a caravan and running around Australia, disappearing from everybody, being a nomad. That was sort of like a major hypothetical because I knew my problems were far more intense than any caravan trip could endure.

Another option for me was to continue being the nutcase that I was, as I was constantly being told I was not making the best decisions. Other people's comments always impact your decision a hell of a lot. Not that they have any right to judge your decisions and how you make them based on your circumstances, but it certainly contributes to making you feel worse.

Well, I didn't realize that how many of the retreats didn't work at that time of year, like February. And I was just so... I don't know, I guess I was really gutted when I called so many of them and didn't get any response, like they didn't hear somebody in

Ultimate Relationship: Part 1

desperate need. They had an answer machine, I'm like, "Why are these people pretending to help and yet they can't even pick up the phone?"

They had an answering machine because they were on holidays, and I was just absolutely gob smacked. I was like, "Where the hell does someone go when they're in doubt?" No wonder so many people go to the hospitals and end up medicated because they are looking for other ways, but these people – don't get me wrong, they have great intentions – don't have the best business plan.

I know they can't help everybody, but to not even give someone a call back? To not even have a person on the other end of the phone? That's what the whole thing is about.

We are the retreat that can help save your life… in so many other words, but that's what I was seeing at the time because I did need someone to save my life: little did I know it was going to be me.

So, I found this retreat said that they specialized in depression and anxiety, and I thought, 'Well, that's perfect.' I had been diagnosed with depression and post-natal depression, so I rang them, and lo-and-behold, they didn't answer. So, I just left the message and I went back to the drawing board as I had to do something. But that night I had a phone call, and it really… I mean, it's really hard to describe the person as per how I thought of him at the time because now I've seen him, and I know how I'd describe him – but back then he seemed

Chapter 8: Running Away

really gentle, and he seemed to know that when people make the call to his retreat they're in dire straits.

Anyway, regardless of that, I had left a message with them and they said I would get a call back, and I did. The minute that I realised where the call was coming from, I broke and balled my eyes out and he said, "Oh, you're really in a bad way, aren't you?" He was making these funny jokes, but I didn't really feel that I had any humorous bones left in my body.

He gave me the options. The money side of it wasn't an issue – I still had some savings from selling my house and stuff, and I knew I needed to spend some money to get the help that I wanted and needed. I really just felt like it was just the right thing to do.

I also made the decision to do this particular retreat. My reasons for choosing the retreats was that they had to be neutral, they couldn't be religious in any way. This one wasn't Christian or Catholic, it was completely neutral. I felt like I was so fucked up at the time anyway that I couldn't wrap my head around someone else's religion that they'd try to push onto me. That was just my thinking at that time.

I guess that the downfall with the retreat was that it was back on the Sunshine coast, and oh my God. I had to then decide what I was going to do, and he says, "Look, if you want to do it, it's up to you, you just put a thousand dollars in the account and I will take your details. That's the deposit and we'll just fix up the rest when you get up here."

Ultimate Relationship: Part 1

So, I talked with my cousin about it. I even called my ex-boyfriend (even though he broke it off with me) to tell him. Oh, how my mind was still very fucked up at that time. Then I had to discuss it with my children. But we were still in that dysfunctional mode; I felt like it had already hit my children so much, I didn't think I could break this news to them. Or to my mum, for that matter, because here my mum thought I had brought the kids and was down here to stay with her, make a new life for myself, and then I was going away again.

I got my cousin to talk to them, and she put it to them as they would go back to their dad while I was going to a retreat for two weeks. They both decided on their own accord that they wanted to stay with their Nonna (my mum) while I was at the retreat. My heart literally broke a little bit, more for them because they could see how I was just not doing well, and they would just... I don't know... they just seemed to do whatever I wanted, I don't know. Maybe one day I'll ask them, but it's one of those things where I think, 'Why would you want to try and get somebody to remember such a horrible painful memory?'

It's really interesting how much emotion is coming up for me right now just by writing about all of this because... I don't know, it's just interesting the amount of emotion.

I was so ashamed that I was going to a retreat as well, because I just felt like I was like one of those addicts, all that jazz. It just wasn't my proudest moment. You don't go shouting it out to the whole world, basically. I couldn't tell their father about this, either.

Chapter 8: Running Away

Anyway, my kids were going to stay with my mum, so I had to enrol them in school and go buy a few things for my trip away. I asked my mum to take me to the airport, and on the way, I asked her, "Can you please just do the drop-off thing? I'm not doing goodbyes today, I'm not doing that. I just need you please to drop me off, and off you go, just keep driving back home." It was just one of the worst emotional moments. I remember I walked up to the check-out, got my tickets, still had my sunglasses on – I think I actually had to take them off because of terrorist scans or, I don't know, whatever – so I lifted them up to show them that I wasn't hiding anything, I was just freaking upset and messed up.

Then, I just went out and sat outside until I needed to go, and I was sobbing to my cousin, "I'm not doing this, I'm not doing this, I don't want to do this." I was just so talking myself out of this. She was just like, "You can do this, you have got to do this." She was my rock – she is my rock – and I just sobbed and told her how much I loved her, and how I was so scared of doing this because I had no idea of what I was in for. I was just so freaking scared.

I left it right up to the last second for me to go through the gates and sit in the waiting area because I didn't want everyone to see me crying. I was wearing the sunglasses inside the airport. I did my sunglasses thing, hopped on the plane with them, didn't know when it was going to stop. As the plane headed for Queensland, I felt like I was going to just throw up everywhere, as I was turning myself inside out. Knowing of what I was stepping into... actually, not knowing.

Ultimate Relationship: Part 1

All I knew is that I booked a ticket to go to this retreat, and I was headed back to Queensland. And here I was on the plane and I just sat there and cried the whole trip.

I was like "Oh my gosh, I'm going be sick, what the fuck am I doing?"

"Can I turn around?"

"Can I get the plane to stop?"

"Can I get the air hostess to let me off?"

I was just contemplating everything...

When I got the Sunshine Coast Airport, two people from retreat were there to collect me. They said they were going to be standing there with my name on it. I got off the plane and I got my luggage; I saw them and I'm like, 'Fuck no, I'm not getting into that goddamn car with them, nope,' and I turned and walked in the opposite direction.

Thoughts in my head were screaming at me:

'I can't believe I'm back on the Sunshine Coast.'

'What the hell am I doing here?'

'Nope, I'm not going; I've seen my name, I know that they're there, that's great, but I'm not quite ready yet.'

I'm actually feeling nauseous trying to remember things right now.

Chapter 8: Running Away

So, I went over to a counter, got a bottle of water, and I think I tried to buy some food even though I didn't feel like eating, as I hadn't eaten much throughout the week. I also hadn't had any alcohol, so there was a lot of withdrawal going on in my body contributing to the fucked-up-ness in my head or my body, whatever.

Once I bought that, I was just like, 'Ok, you paid your deposit, there they're waiting for you, you bought your water, you've tried to run away, you've tried to stop this process; but now you got to just step into this, Ria, and do this, it's what you've gotta do, you've got no other choice.'

I went up to them and said, "Hey, I'm Ria." There was a young guy and a tall guy, and they went, "Ok." I guess that they were quite used to the state in which people rocked up to them when they picked them up, you know, based on other people's situations and them thinking that they were at the end of their road, like me. So, they just asked me some basic questions, but I was really quite short. I was just saying single words, like, "No, maybe, yep, nothing." I didn't even want to talk. I was just like, 'what the fuck?' So, they ended up just talking between themselves, while I was sitting in the back of the car crying my heart out.

Chapter 9: At the Retreat

Chapter 9: At the Retreat

When I was at the airport, I was still crying, and the two guys that picked me up asked me basic questions, I guess they'd been doing this for a while and wanted to know my state of mind. To know where the people are at when they're actually entering the retreat. I just remember me being in full-on defence mode, looking at one of the guys and going, "Oh my God, what the hell do you know?" You know, I'm pretty much known for saying things the way I see them, and I just said it out loud, no filter. "What the hell would you know?" And he didn't comment, he didn't retaliate, he didn't react. I can't tell you if he responded. I know we had a chuckle at the end of the retreat and a few times afterwards where we'd met up.

This guy had gone through some significant things from the age of 13 and here I am judging him based on how he looked, or the age of him. It brings a lot of stuff into perspective now, based on what I know.

Anyway, so they took me to the retreat and I looked at my surroundings. I was in the middle of the back of Maleny, in the country, about 15-minute drive from the suburb. I was thinking, "What the hell have I done? What am I doing here?"

I was absolutely disgusted with myself. How did I let it get this far? Why am I here? Why did I step into this?

Still crying, still had my sunglasses on for whatever reason, I think I believed that nobody could see that I was crying, but everybody else that had been there for weeks before me obviously had an idea how you look when you rock up, and how you look when you go home.

Ultimate Relationship: Part 1

So, I had a meeting with the boss lady, and she took me through the orientation process. She asked me a few questions regarding where I was at and told me how the program worked. I was talking about the whole detox part of it because to detox your mind you have to clear out the toxins, which you get from food, alcohol and other substances… which was a strange thing because in the week before I'd gone to the retreat I'd probably had maybe one drink, because I was just so absolutely dysfunctional, and to be honest the reason for me drinking back then was to numb the pain. It didn't matter if I had a drink or a whole bottle, it didn't do the same job anymore.

Whatever was working once upon a time wasn't freaking working now. So, the whole food program was all about detox – detox from dairy, detox from wheat, detox from gluten, detox from sugar, detox from caffeine, detox from alcohol. It was about putting really good foods into your body. I had already been living in so much fear of what I was putting into my mouth, so that's what that aspect of the program was about.

There was also a juicing program which I was quite interested in – not for a weight loss factor, just because it can really strip all of those toxins a lot faster; however, I realized from talking to this lady that my body was almost in shut down mode because of the lack of nutrients I was putting into it, because of that state of mind I was in at that time. It was fully dehydrated at that time – if you pinched my skin, it just stayed there. She actually advised me to not to do the juicing part

Chapter 9: At the Retreat

because I really needed to get some nutrients back in my body, and I guess another aspect now that I'm talking about it was to trust in food again and trust the benefits of what it can do for me.

Unbeknownst to me, I had no idea of the rewards I'd get from doing what I did – I'll tell you more about that later in the chapter.

So, I had that chat, and was shown to my room. There were all these little cabins, but I found out later on in the program that the rooms inside the house were for people that were on watch for whatever reason, and I was being put in one of the rooms in the house.

Let me try to give you a visual of what the place looked like: it was set on a mountain in the country. There was this massive farm house, with an office and kitchen at the front, a big dining room on the veranda, and then inside was a communal lounge room. Inside there on that level there were two massive bedrooms with en-suites, then there was two other bedrooms and a bathroom that they and every other guest could use. Downstairs there was the laundry, storage, and a massage room – I think there were actually two massage rooms, from memory – and then there was also the big room where we went to our group sessions and stuff like that.

I don't know if I made it sound really nice or not. It was very nice, but at that time I wasn't really looking at the beauty that was in the world because I didn't know about it, I didn't feel it

Ultimate Relationship: Part 1

inside of me. That's a massive, massive realization, which I will tell you a little story about later on.

Anyway, I got shown to my room, which was lovely. It was just this king-sized bed, all done up nice. So, I just sat on the bed and was crying, crying, crying, and then this other lady came in. She happened to be the yoga teacher there, and she's like, "Are you alright?" And I'm like, "No, no I'm not." I told her my life story in a matter of minutes because it was so worthwhile, cried some more, and thought, 'What am I to do right now? I don't know.'

Then, one of the life coaches there came and had to ask me – debrief me – like my medical issues, basically check my mental state of mind.

I just laid it all on the table... at that point in time I had just paid a huge amount of money to get to this place, I had nowhere else to go in my mind, absolutely nowhere, except possibly to a padded cell in a psych ward. So, why not just freaking lay all on the table. I certainly hadn't been honest to any of the counsellors or psychologists in the last 10 years regarding my feeling in the suicidal gauge or anything like that. I was not quite suicidal at that moment, but don't get me wrong... so, why not just get it all out and be done with it, get the help that you freaking well need, Ria. That's why I did it; I was just laying it all out.

As I did that, obviously more tears came out, and she was like, "Do you want something to eat?" I was like, "No." Apparently, I was being monitored about what I was eating for the next 3

Chapter 9: At the Retreat

days or however, I don't know how long I was being monitored, or even if I was, maybe that was a fabrication in my own mind. I felt like I was being watched. I was asked a number of times if I had meals and stuff like that because I didn't actually eat at the communal table with everybody else, I was too ashamed to be sitting with a bunch of people. I don't know, I just didn't want to see anybody, I didn't want to talk to anybody, I guess except for the help that I had paid for.

So, that's what I did. I'd go and get my food, I'd come into my room and I'd eat it, I didn't know if I was allowed to or not, but that's exactly what I did. I took my plates back, I did all the right things, I always tried to do. I got there on the Friday afternoon (Valentine's Day, 2014), and I pretty much just cried myself to sleep listening to or watching YouTube videos.

I was a smoker, and I had spoken to one of the coaches because I didn't know if I could go out. I didn't know if the people were safe to be able to go out and have a cigarette around next to them and have a smoke. That was just my insecurity, and who knows, maybe they were or not, I don't know who they were, I didn't know. My fears were just so ramped, the paranoia that I was experiencing in those moments was phenomenal, and the way I felt right in that moment I never will go back to. I can say that now, I didn't know that then.

That weekend was one of the most emotional I've ever experienced. I couldn't tell you what they were actually talking about, but basically, I had a 3-day intensive workshop as soon

Ultimate Relationship: Part 1

as I got there, which is, to a lot of people, freaking harsh. But, they know this program, they've been doing it for years, and so I just did what they said.

I was given a program of where I was meant to be and when. When I was looking at my program, it said, "6 o'clock walk", and so I got up at 6 o'clock and went for a walk with one of the ladies (I think she was a helper in the kitchen, and I think the yoga teacher actually went with her, and it was me, and another lady that was also there as a patient/client). I remember being on this walk, crying again as I went, that was just my new-found hobby, I guess. One thing I guess I didn't realize about it at that time, was this intuition thing. This lady and I got talking about things, and I was just angry, and I'm like, "I'm so freaking angry!" And she goes, "Oh, no you're not, there's such a sadness within you." And I was almost screaming at her telling her how freaking angry I was.

I think she just left it obviously, she wasn't going to keep on arguing the point with me. Now I just find that quite hilarious because over the course of those two weeks I realised how freaking sad I was. The tears didn't come up because I was angry – the angry was just masking the emotion sitting under it.

The intensive went on to Monday. A lot of things are such a blur, as you can tell from the last chapter; I remember sitting in the classes and there was a lot of stuff going on that was just triggering me. The coach that was running the classes like, when I was listening to what she was saying it just was

Chapter 9: At the Retreat

triggering me left, right and centre. When I say trigger, for me a trigger is all the emotion that it brings up, it causes me to react inside. She was telling me these things, like that I was creating my universe, and I'm like, "Oh my gosh, no, no, this is not possible!" Every single molecule in my body over that weekend was fighting against what she was telling me, because I had finally made the decision to make a goddamn change in my life. I could feel it, it was gut wrenching, it was heart wrenching, it made me furious. This other client there was getting quite frustrated and angry, and it was setting me off inside, and I had to walk out of the classroom because I couldn't handle his violent outburst that freaked the life out of me. I couldn't understand why, I just couldn't deal with it. I could hear when he walked out at one stage (because I was like a yo-yo and kept leaving the class and coming back), I had calmed down from seeing that violent outburst.

He was not violent towards everybody, just in case that person happens to read my book, and he may not even know that I'm talking about him.

The whole intensive program just pushed me to my limit, set my triggers off in such a way that whenever this coach came towards me, she knew that I was obviously feeling very emotional because all I did was freaking cry there. She would come up to me and say, "Are you ok?" And I couldn't even answer it because I knew that if I answered her I'd be a heaving mess, and I mean it.

Ultimate Relationship: Part 1

I was almost hyperventilating, crying at that moment, in my own silent way. I just remember her, she's such a beautiful woman, and she was not doing anything to harm me, or anything like that, she was just trying to teach me this program. When I say program... the program was, in short, telling me that life doesn't have to be the way that it was, there was a whole another way to live. And for me to have gone 33 years of living one way, and then get told there is a whole goddamn another way of living?

Do you know how fucking angry it makes you feel?

It's almost like if you've been living a lie.

Who the fuck is responsible for that?

Why didn't somebody tell me how to live properly?

Actually live, not just exist in the world. The only person freaking responsible is me. And so be it, for everybody else in this world, that's it, there is nobody else responsible, it is nobody else's fault that I didn't get taught this shit. I chose to live my life the way I lived based on what I knew at the time.

The next three days consisted of classes, learning about meditation, and I'm like, 'Holy crap... meditation, I'm not learning that voodoo crap, what the hell?' However, once again, the whole process of meditation was nothing like what I had been taught. Shame on the people that say it's some other thing, to be honest. When I was learning about meditation they just took me places to just try and be still and breathe. However, I was only breathing from the neck up. I

Chapter 9: At the Retreat

know that sounds completely incorrect, anatomically incorrect and all that jazz, but quite frankly that's how I was breathing, and you'll find out the reasons why. But, when you're in fight-or-flight mode for God knows how many years of your life you don't breathe indeed, you can't, it's a complete impossibility really, at least for me. I shouldn't talk for anybody else, but for me it was a completely impossibility.

I did this meditation where I looked into a candle and tried to be still with my thoughts, which were still circling like a mad woman… not even circling, I don't know, like a washing machine operating as fast as it can go, spinning around in my head, making my guts cringe and boil, and everything else. But not only did I have all my shit from before that was circling, I had all this new stuff on top of that to fuck all of that other shit up, and I was like, 'I don't know if I can actually do this shit, I think I need to go, I think I made a really, really, really bad mistake coming here because I don't know if I can fully function doing this.'

There was a session one afternoon and it was a group class where the coach asked questions. I didn't hold back in any way. I sat there quietly and cried for most of it, writing down every single thing, I was like a sponge, just learning about all of these new ways of thinking. They were talking about experiences that had happened in their lives. I had no hesitation in voicing those to get this new perspective on how it could've been different, or to try and change my thought process about it.

Ultimate Relationship: Part 1

I remember sitting there in one of the sessions with a different coach, and she had said at the beginning that she used to run the program, but also depending on the group at the time she could bring the modalities into the process. Which, I had no fucking clue what she was really on about, I didn't even know what a modality was. It was one of those things that you hang around your neck or something? Seriously? Anyway, as the class progressed she told us the story of her own life, when she was in a Catholic school and she was given limited toilet paper to go the toilet and how that was for her in her life. So, she gave us two squares of toilet paper and we had to write all of the shame, everything that we didn't want to tell anybody, and none of us wanted to lift up a pen. I think there was about 10 of us in the room, and nobody wanted to lift up a pen until she said "Look, nobody has to read those out, it is literally between you and your piece of toilet paper, and when you're finished writing them all down, you're literally letting it go." It was a "let go" process I guess, not that I really knew what a process was either at that time.

And you're probably thinking, 'Fuck, this Ria woman is crazy, she keeps talking about all these things, but she didn't even know what they were!' It's just that I've done loads of work, and it'll all come to pass through reading the course of this book.

We wrote down everything; I think everybody filled up their little two pieces of toilet paper squares front and back once we realized we didn't have to disclose any of the information to anybody. And as we did so, the tears were flowing for some

Chapter 9: At the Retreat

of us. Then she took us upstairs to the lounge near the fireplace, and we lit them and put them all into the fire.

Oh my God, seriously, to be able to even acknowledge all of those things in that form is so empowering, because even if you don't have the ability to say the words out loud, when you put pen to paper it just comes out. It was a really, really, really massive experience, not just for me, but for the other people in that room as well.

I think the coach had asked to say a few things to each other. We went back downstairs and did this thing where we partnered up with someone in the room, and we had to give them an empowering word that we felt embodied that person. Once that person was told the word we thought reflected them, that person had to claim it and say, "I am courageous." And I was like, "I don't know who you think you are, but you don't know me. I'm not courageous in any way."

Then, as we did that process I'm like, "Seriously, my throat is blocked up." When they told me I was courageous I was completely beside myself, I had snot dribbling out of my nose, the tears couldn't flow fast enough from my eyes, and this is all in the same process after writing down all those shameful things I felt in my life.

I could not put that word next to "I am", I couldn't, except I did. As I said the words, "I AM courageous," I was brought to my knees, hyperventilating and crying. I don't know if people know what that is, but... my body was just totally in upheaval mode, big time.

Ultimate Relationship: Part 1

After that process, the coach saw something in me, it was like a switch or something that she saw, and she went, "Ok, that switch is on now, I've got to go to another process." She came over to me and said, "We're going to go to another process right now, we're going to have a one on one coaching session." I went, "Ok, alright."

"Are you ready?"

"Yeah."

'No', but there I was, following her.

I went into my room with her, I laid on the bed as she sat beside me, and she talked me into this restful space. I really didn't have much of an idea of what was really taking place, but she goes, "Ok, so where are your triggers right now?" And in this process, she took me to meet my fear, basically.

So, where she took me to first was where the fear stung me, with my boyfriend. I talked about that and the situation there, about how we moved into a house and my boyfriend was moving furniture out of the truck and the leg of the desk collapsed, and he grabbed the desk; he threw the desk. He grabbed it out, I don't know if he was pissed off, he was probably exhausted, I don't know, but he grabbed that desk and threw it on the ground in such a way that it scared the living daylights out of me.

I could not explain how it made me feel inside because I had no fucking clue what the hell was going on. So, people asked me, "Why don't you talk about it?" "Why don't you talk about

Chapter 9: At the Retreat

what was going on for you before the retreat?" "You could've saved yourself some bucks?" ... No fucking way.

How can I explain something to somebody or anybody if I can't even understand or make sense of it myself? Because all I could feel was something going on inside of me, something was churning, something didn't feel right.

Then the life coach said, "Ok, now take me back to the time it happened before."

So that was with my brother, and a number of times, it wasn't just one moment that was triggered inside of me, but my brother and I used to have some pretty volatile verbal arguments. Reflection, reflection, but as we were in the middle of this particular disagreement, argument, whatever you want to call it... I remember picturing him in the doorway of the bathroom and I was standing there, and I was scared out of my brains. Not because I believed he was going to hurt me, but he was taller than me, and he was a lot bigger than me, and as he was yelling at me that feeling inside of me was growing again. I was not pregnant either, in case you just hopped into the book at this page. That thing was stirring inside of me again, and it was making me feel not good. I stood my ground and I was not going to back out of this fight because that's just not what I did. I did not back out. Regardless of how it made me feel inside, I just stood my ground, and this feeling just started to explode inside of me.

Then the coach said, "Ok, take me back to the next time." And the next time was with my ex-husband; there were a few times

Ultimate Relationship: Part 1

with him, we had pretty interesting disagreements, arguments, but I just remembered a couple of times, I don't really know what they were about. I was standing in the kitchen one time, I don't remember if I had both my kids at that time, but he was so angry for whatever reason, probably something I said to tip him off (I did a lot of that at the time, I would trigger other people as well, though not on purpose). As I was standing in the kitchen in this particular moment, he found some scissors that I believe my daughter had.

(This is quite difficult, because I had to go through times in my life that quite frankly I didn't want to remember).

Standing in the kitchen, he found this pair of scissors in my daughters hand and he was fuming; apparently because I had allowed her to touch them, and it was all my fault. Who knows, the conversation could've gone completely different... all I can remember in this moment was the blame that I was getting, the blame for the fact I had allowed my daughter to have a pair of scissors in her hand, which I do not believe was the case. He grabbed the scissors off my daughter, and he flung them towards my direction... I don't know if he was aiming at me, I don't think so, but they landed in the sink, but he threw it with such force that it actually pierced a hole straight through my sink. You can gauge the ferocity of that throw. Then they bounced out and luckily landed on the bench and not anywhere else.

Then, there was another time that freaked me out and caused my inside feeling to just go wild. I can't tell you what the

Chapter 9: At the Retreat

argument was because I don't remember, but he grabbed the car keys – we were standing outside the bedroom we were going off at each other – and threw them at the wall, and when he threw them at the wall they literally grazed the wall.

People could say, "Oh, that's domestic violence, that's this, that's that," you know what, fuck that shit. I'm not going into that kind of label, that kind of emotional victimhood for the sake of saving my own life, because at the end of the day, for me, there were so many things that I was contributing to myself, that was a part of it as well. So, if I'm going to call domestic violence on this situation, then I call it on myself. Whether you choose to agree with me or not that's not for me to decide, that's how I feel about it and that's all that matters.

Then, as the process continued...

I was deep in this process... basically she asked me to take her back to the time it first happened, and when I did that...

I was so opened to the fact that I just wanted to shift whatever started all of this in the beginning. It was really easy for me to just... I felt very safe and I felt very supported, so I just dropped straight into where it first started, where I was able to go back to a very young age, around three, which a lot of stuff happened at that age.

It was my dad, to my knowledge there was no physical violence to me, but he was so violent with his words. I remember this one incident where he had gotten so angry.

Ultimate Relationship: Part 1

A little recap on my Dad; he wasn't really there for me as a young kid, he wasn't there for me as a father, he used to work in his bakery all the time, and that was ok like that, that was his thing. It wasn't ok for me however, I wanted my dad more in my life, it just didn't seem to be like that.

This is just the memory that I have, and I want to make sure it's written that it's my memory, not anybody else's, because as I've learned we all have a very, very different memory – even if we're looking at the same thing, we can have a very different visual of what we see or what we perceive; our perception is very, very different.

Back to the point. To my knowledge, he'd just got home from work and he had fallen asleep on the lounge. My brother was two and a half years younger than me, and we were playing, and there was a vacuum, I was sitting on top of the vacuum and I thought it was a horse – I was about three. My brother was barely crawling, and I thought that the vacuum was the horse and carriage. I picked up the cord and I wrapped it around my brother's neck. Not the best thing, but you know what, I was a kid, I didn't freaking know any different, we were playing a game, I had no idea of consequences or that I could actually hurt somebody, and not that I had any intention of hurting him. We were just playing a fun game as kids do, and my dad saw this, and when he arose from his nap on the lounge and he went off his tree. He was yelling, he was screaming, I couldn't tell what he was yelling and screaming about except for the fact that he saw me and my brother playing a game, and he didn't like it. I don't know if this

Chapter 9: At the Retreat

particular incident resulted in the two holes in my bedroom door, or the two holes in the bathroom door, or the ones in the laundry.

That just triggered another memory for me, which was... I believe it was my sister's birthday. He came home to bring in the birthday cake for her birthday, and we had a huge amount of people there, probably just family really. We had a dog, a Labrador called Sunny, and when he brought the cake out, the dog had a party hat on because my brother thought it would be really sweet to include the dog in the party. Once again, we were kids, we didn't know what party hats could do with a strip of elastic. It had actually cut through his neck and he had a strip of blood around his neck, and my dad went nuts again.

Once again, I visually remember holes in the laundry door; was that because of that party? I don't know.

But that fear that was instilled in me at that time created havoc throughout my life. I was in this process, there was power in being able to go back to specific times in my life and be able to hit the nail on the head. This is not putting blame on my father, just to be clear, it just started things in my life and created a pattern of behaviour for me.

When I was able to realize that and understand where it came from, I was able to then forgive myself – not just forgive my father, but to forgive him for where he was in his life, and also to forgive myself for taking all this guilt and fear onto my shoulder which wasn't even mine to take on.

Ultimate Relationship: Part 1

I didn't know at the age of three what was and what wasn't, and you know, I forgave myself for the blame, because I was being blamed at that time. I was giving myself that peace to just be able to go, "I didn't know any different at that time, now that I'm 36 years old, I know different."

When I was doing the process, I was 33 years old, and to be able to take on that amount of guilt and blame for 30 years is a phenomenal thing. And I don't believe enough of us are taught to forgive ourselves for things that we didn't know at that time. There's no blame in that, there's no guilt in that; however, that's how society gives it to us.

Anyway, the minute that I was able to see that fear and realize where it came from, I felt utter relief. I felt for the first time in my life that I could feel my own heart beating inside my chest. I know that, clearly, to all the scientists out there, my heart was beating in my chest. However, I had so much guilt and blame there, it was sitting on top of my heart, it was sitting inside my intestines where I had a disease growing within me and poisoning me. This fear, this blame and this guilt was killing me, but all of a sudden, after I had found this deep-seated fear, blame, and guilt, I just felt so relieved, and so… there is no other word, just utter relief, I just felt so light, I felt like I was in the clouds.

It felt amazing. From that pivotal moment, every single thing changed for me, the pain that I had felt for 9 months within my diagnosis of Crohns Disease had dissipated.

Chapter 9: At the Retreat

Maybe that was because of the food that I was eating in the retreat, which was completely organic and natural, not influenced by caffeine, alcohol, sugar, wheat or gluten, or because I was willing to go beyond any length that I've ever gone to before, and really dug deep into myself. Just dug deep and finally heal the parts of me that was willing to be healed, once and for all. Who knows? I think, personally, it was a contribution of all of that. The willingness of me even wanting to go to retreat in the first place, the willingness of me stepping into the unknown and feeling freaking scared but doing it anyway. It was hugely powerful. The end of my retreat was just amazing.

I just turned into a sponge for the remainder of my retreat process, and I've got other paper work and stuff, everything that I learned there, which was total CBT, cognitive behaviour therapy… so, that's me and the retreat. We'll just go to the next chapter, which will be what happened after the retreat.

Chapter 10: Life After the Retreat

Chapter 10: Life After the Retreat

As I write this last chapter about my life after the retreat, I just finished a podcast with a beautiful lady, basically talking about my story and how I just feel even more inspired to get my book completed. I figured I might as well talk about the last chapter of my book, and how I was trying to get it all completed. The last chapter of my book is about when I left the retreat.

Although I feared the unknown, I was grateful for everything I learned in the two weeks, and to be able to put that into action and to be able to stand on my own two feet. Not that I really hadn't during my life prior to that, but with all this newfound stuff that I've learned about myself and what I've been taught, it was pretty daunting.

I flew home from the retreat and went back to Sydney to see my children and my family. I got there, and I was so grateful for my mum to have looked after my children, my husband, and my family who rallied around me at a time when I couldn't even explain to them what the hell was going on.

I had asked for their hand, and they had stepped up, they were there for me. I will forever ever be grateful for everything that they have supported me with and encouraged me with, because they're my family, and I love them for it.

I got back down there and started doing life differently. As I went for walks and listened to some of my meditations, I realised that I had to go back to the course, to the Sunshine Coast, where my home had been for 18 years. There were so many loose ends that I had to go and tie up, all that unfinished business. I had burnt so many bridges.

Ultimate Relationship: Part 1

It wasn't that I felt guilty for doing that, as I don't believe I can't feel guilty for how I felt in that particular time in my life when everything was spiralling out of control. However, I could at least make amends for some of my actions, and to do so, I packed up my kids and moved back to the coast.

I didn't have a house to go to,

I didn't have a job,

I had my kids.

From learning everything I'd learned in the retreat, I had this new sense, this new foundation of "It is going to be ok."

I had to just trust in everything that I've done in my life, and also trust in the universe, to trust in what the universe can bring me. Some people choose to call that higher power God, or all kinds of different things. I choose to call that power higher than myself the universe. I don't want to get into arguments with anyone, that's just what it is for me.

I had to really step it up a notch and say, "Universe, I am just going to trust in what is going to happen now, trust in what you're going to bring forth for me, and I'm going to step up."

Obviously, because I felt I had burnt so many bridges, I joined a few meetup groups and connections through Facebook groups and stuff. I needed to step outside of my parent circle that I been in. I felt that I just needed to meet some new people, and that was one of the scariest things I've ever done… to walk into a room and not know a single person, have to

Chapter 10: Life After the Retreat

introduce yourself, say why you're there and whatever. I don't know if they asked me that question, I'm certain they asked me my name.

I had gotten rid of that mentality, that belief system that it was all black and white and I can trust no one but myself.

In reality, from what I had learned, that was the furthest thing from the truth. It is absolutely the furthest thing from the truth. When I started to trust and to step outside of my own comfort circle, meet new people, everything in my world just opened up.

I joined a little meditation circle, it makes me laugh every time I say that word. Because I had been told so many things about meditation, how bad it was, how evil it was, and so many different connotations to it.

I've stepped into my little "woo-woo" land, I'm fully in my woo-woo land now. I don't think there would be one person that could actually convince me otherwise because, quite frankly, I'm the happiest I've ever been in my life.

It's not perfect, it's far from that, but I have the peace inside of me from soul searching within myself, and finding my peace, finding my happy. Finding my own joy has brought me so much happiness, more that I could've ever, ever believed.

I found it in myself first – and that would have to be the most astounding find in my whole life, bigger than I could've ever hoped for. Realizing that and stepping outside of my own comfort zone and stepping into groups where I knew nobody,

Ultimate Relationship: Part 1

stepping into self-development courses that brought me closer to myself, took me to whole new levels of trust, love – mainly trust. At the end of the day, the more I trusted myself, the more the higher power, the universe kept on giving back to me.

One of my moments when I got back from the retreat was when I found my new little home to live in, and it was a little unit in King's Beach. It was old, but as I was standing on the balcony I felt at home, I felt there was no other place like home, like Dorothy from The Wizard of Oz.

When I could smell that ocean coming through the air waves to my unit, I could lie in bed at night and smell the ocean and hear the waves crashing as I slept...

I knew without a doubt that I was home.

One night, shortly after I was back, the father of my kids asked me if he could take my children to a party that he'd been invited to. It was my sister's party. Keep in mind that I had been estranged from my sister for years at this stage.

Prior to me making changes in my life, I actually hadn't been speaking with her, or a number of my siblings, for about four years. I thought about it, and I thought, "No, I don't want them to go, I didn't want my siblings to see my children." I didn't think that they deserved that.

After everything that had transpired, my new way of thinking kicked in... 'Well, if you're going to continue thinking like you

Chapter 10: Life After the Retreat

always did, then nothing is going to change, you have got to step up, Ria.' Call me crazy...

I was talking to myself, and you know what, I have had the best freaking conversations with myself, it's been amazing. I get so much clarity when I talk to myself. I'll put my hand up if anyone wants to call me whatever they want to call me, "Yeah, I talk to myself."

So, my decision was yes, they can go to this event with their father, with my sister there. When they got home, the joy on my kids' faces pretty much brought tears to my eyes for so many different reasons, because it made me realize how much I still loved my family, not that I ever believed that I didn't, but holy moly the emotions coming up right now.

It made me realize how much I loved my family, and no matter what transpired,

you can't change love,

it's just there.

Then my kids told me that my sister was pregnant, then I had all these other emotions running through me because I felt like, 'fucking hell, Ria! You idiot! You cut them off because of some petty little things', even though it felt like the biggest turmoil in my life.

I felt like I started to beat myself up about it because I hadn't seen my sister for so long and here she was with this new man,

Ultimate Relationship: Part 1

she was engaged, she had a business, and she was pregnant, and I'm just sitting back and I am missing out on that.

My new way of thinking kicked in again and said, 'Ria, you didn't miss out on anything because you can't miss out on something ever, it's a fallacy, it's a myth that we tell ourselves so we can upset ourselves and feel like we're stuck on the outer, it's just a horrible thing that we do to ourselves.'

The next day I actually wrote a message to my sister after all this happened. I couldn't send it at that time because it was bringing up a lot of emotion. I started writing it, and after my children had gone to see my sister, my sister wrote me a message through Facebook. I don't really know how it came through because I had, when I felt so betrayed years before, blocked my sister, and most of my siblings at that time. Somehow, the universe prevailed as it always does, and I had this message from my sister, and, basically it was just telling me how much she loved me, and she was sorry for everything that happened, that now was a time to move forward and let all that go.

In that moment, I felt like it was the right time to send mine, which was pretty much exactly the same words from me to her. I cried, and I cried for days knowing that I had stepped out of my comfort zone and I opened myself up to trusting in the universe and bringing forth more joy, why not? Like, "Hello, this is my life to live now."

I'm getting really emotional again because when I started talking we decided to meet up again and she was pregnant...

Chapter 10: Life After the Retreat

it brought so much joy to me to see her being pregnant, and now I'm a part of her life, which I always really was. I just had a few gap years... I'm just so grateful to myself to have her back in my life.

There were just so many moments like this when I kept on stepping up. Basically, I enrolled in a study course for a business diploma. I decided to do a double business diploma, because I had so much experience in businesses that I really wanted to back it up with the background knowledge for everything that I already knew. Even though I knew so much and had so much experience, there was a hell of a lot to learn on the flipside of what happens behind the scenes of a business. I also did it, to be honest, to meet some more people.

Once again, I met three beautiful souls – actually four, I connected with another one at the end of my business diploma, we still call out for coffee and have gone out in a few times together. I just connected with them so well, it was such a lovely experience to go through that journey with them. Here I was trying to make new friends, I ended up with new friends and the double business diploma, how lucky can I get?

Then, I also got accepted for a scholarship. Well, I actually applied for a job and ended up getting a scholarship to Flight Centre, and I did a Certificate II in Tourism. I also did a Certificate IV in small business management. Then I decided also that I would finish my children's education diploma. Because of my experience in my day-care, I got most of it RPL'd

Ultimate Relationship: Part 1

(Recognized Prior Learning), and I only had to do a couple of units that were not covered by my experience.

I was getting to the end of 2014, and I realized that I had opened so many doors, I had literally opened all the communications back home with my family. I wasn't working all that much, but I was working one to two shifts a week. I was still raising my children, watching them grow and change, and hearing them tell me how hippy I was getting. It makes me laugh because of everything that I learned at retreat about labels and perceptions. Whenever they called me a hippie I sort of giggled to myself. I think about the word Hippy and think, "What does that actually constitute? If my kids see me as a hippie, what does that mean?" It brought so much joy to my life.

At the end of the year I started doing samba dancing, and I think doing that and also a self-development course into the inner child aspects of yourself, that really rocked my world, that took me to a much deeper part of myself that I guess I never thought I would face.

However, I believe that by doing all the work I had done, and filling my head with good data, information that fed my soul, and me looking after myself once and for all, it was time to heal.

And heal and grow is exactly what I did. Find out what happened next in *Ultimate Relationship: Part 2*.

THE END

www.ingramcontent.com/pod-product-compliance
Lightning Source LLC
Chambersburg PA
CBHW071724090426
42738CB00009B/1865